Twisted Classics

edited by
JEANNE STAUFFER &
SANDRA L. HATCH

HOUSE of WHITE BIRCHES

PUBLISHERS
SINCE 1947

Twisted Classics

Editors: Jeanne Stauffer, Sandra L. Hatch

Art Director: Brad Snow

Publishing Services Manager: Brenda Gallmeyer

Associate Editor: Dianne Schmidt

Assistant Art Director: Nick Pierce

Copy Supervisor: Michelle Beck

Copy Editors: Nicki Lehman, Mary O'Donnell, Beverly Richardson

Technical Artist: Connie Rand

Graphic Arts Supervisor: Ronda Bechinski

Book Design: Edith Teegarden

Graphic Artist: Debby Keel

Production Assistants: Cheryl Kempf, Marj Morgan, Judy Neuenschwander

Photography: Tammy Christian, Don Clark, Matthew Owen, Jackie Schaffel

Photo Stylists: Tammy Nussbaum, Tammy M. Smith

Publishing Director: David McKee

Marketing Director: Dan Fink

Printed in China

First Printing: 2006

Library of Congress Control Number: 2006922915

Hardcover ISBN-10: 1-59217-127-3
Hardcover ISBN-13: 978-159217-127-9
Softcover ISBN-10: 1-59217-128-1
Softcover ISBN-13: 978-1-59217-128-6

Every effort has been made to ensure the accuracy and completeness of the instructions in this book. However, we cannot be responsible for human error or for the results when using materials other than those specified in the instructions, or for variations in individual work.

1 2 3 4 5 6 7 8 9

Welcome

The 34 unique quilt patterns included in this collection are original designs created by combining two or more traditional quilt block patterns or by manipulating an individual quilt block.

These creative quilt patterns happen when two or more classic blocks are combined in an unusual way that creates a new and unexpected design. One block could be superimposed on top of another block, making a new block altogether. Or the twist is created with the use of careful color placement or unique placement of two or more blocks within the quilt setting.

The twist can also happen within one block by changing its shape, making it taller, fatter, skinnier or wherever the imagination can take you. Then take these out-of-shape blocks and combine them together or with a second familiar block.

The talented designers of the quilts in this book have let their creativity go wild, giving you imaginative patterns to enjoy. The starting point of the quilt might have been a familiar block, but they twisted and turned that block so wonderful new designs that are fun to make would appear.

Information on the way each block is twisted or combined is included, along with easy-to-follow instructions, full-color photos of quilts on beds and straight-on shots of quilts.

The quilts range from easy to advanced in level of difficulty. In addition to large bed quilt designs, there are table runners, wall quilts and throws waiting for your quilting pleasure.

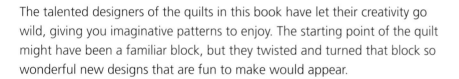

Contents

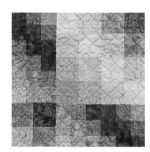

design by **HOLLY DANIELS**

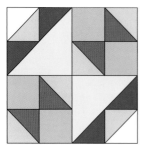

Blue School Girl's Puzzle
12" x 12" Block
Make 4

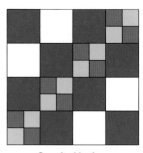

Carrie Nation
12" x 12" Block
Make 8

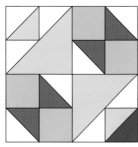

White School Girl's Puzzle
12" x 12" Block
Make 4

Morning Glorious

Change the colors in the corners of the School Girl's Puzzle block and stitch them together to form a pieced flower in the center of this wall quilt. Use Carrie Nation blocks to form a walkway around the center flower design, and you have a fabric garden.

PROJECT SPECIFICATIONS

Skill Level: Intermediate
Quilt Size: 60" x 60"
Block Size: 12" x 12"
Number of Blocks: 16

MATERIALS

- ⅓ yard light yellow mottled
- ½ yard dark yellow check
- ⅝ yard light green mottled
- ⅝ yard dark green tonal
- ¾ yard cream solid
- ⅞ yard dark blue print
- 1⅝ yards blue-and-yellow print
- Backing 66" x 66"

- Batting 66" x 66"
- All-purpose thread to match fabrics
- Quilting thread
- Basic sewing tools and supplies

CUTTING

Step 1. Cut three cream solid A strips and six dark blue print B strips 3½" by fabric width.

Step 2. Cut four 2" by fabric width strips light green mottled (C) and dark green tonal (D).

Step 3. Cut four 6⅞" x 6⅞" squares each dark yellow check (E) and light yellow mottled (K); cut each square in half on one diagonal to make eight each E and K triangles.

Step 4. Cut two 3⅞" by fabric width strips each

dark yellow check (G) and dark green tonal (I); subcut strips into (16) 3⅞" squares each fabric. Cut each square in half on one diagonal to make 32 each G and I triangles.

Step 5. Cut one 3⅞" by fabric width strip dark blue print; subcut strip into (10) 3⅞" squares. Cut each square in half on one diagonal to make 20 J triangles.

Step 6. Cut three 3⅞" by fabric width strips cream solid; subcut strips into (22) 3⅞" squares. Cut each square in half on one diagonal to make 44 F triangles.

Step 7. Cut three 3½" by fabric width strips light green mottled; subcut strips into (32) 3½" H squares.

Step 8. Cut six 6½" by fabric width strips blue-and-yellow print. Join strips on short ends to make one long strip. Subcut strip into two 48½" L strips and two 60½" M strips.

Step 9. Cut six 2¼" by fabric width strips blue-and-yellow print for binding.

COMPLETING THE CARRIE NATION BLOCKS

Step 1. Sew an A strip to a B strip with right sides together along length; press seams toward B. Repeat for three A-B strip sets.

Step 2. Subcut strip sets into (32) 3½" A-B segments as shown in Figure 1.

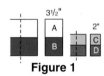

Figure 1

Step 3. Subcut the remaining B strips into (32) 3½" B squares.

Step 4. Sew a C strip to a D strip with right sides together along length; press seams toward D. Repeat for four strip sets.

Step 5. Subcut strip sets into (64) 2" C-D segments, again referring to Figure 1.

Step 6. Join two A-B segments to make an A-B unit as shown in Figure 2; repeat to make 32 units. Press seams in one direction.

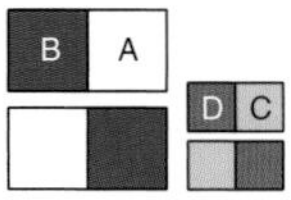

Figure 2

Step 7. Join two C-D segments to make a C-D unit, again referring to Figure 2; repeat for 32 units. Press seams in one direction.

Step 8. To complete one Carrie Nation block, sew a B square to a C-D unit as shown in Figure 3; press seam toward B. Repeat to make four B-C-D units.

Figure 3   **Figure 4**

Step 9. Join two B-C-D units as shown in Figure 4 to complete a corner unit; press seam in one direction. Repeat to make two corner units.

Step 10. Join a corner unit with an A-B unit to make a row as shown in Figure 5; repeat for two rows. Press seams toward A-B units.

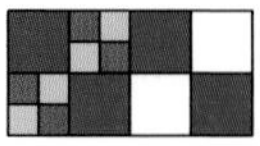

Figure 5

Step 11. Join the rows referring to the block drawing to complete one block; press seams in one direction. Repeat to make eight blocks.

COMPLETING THE WHITE SCHOOL GIRL'S PUZZLE BLOCKS

Step 1. Referring to Figure 6, sew F to I, F to G and G to J; press seams toward I, G and J.

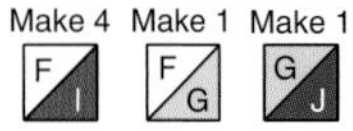

Figure 6 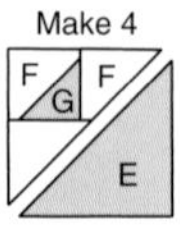   **Figure 7**

Step 2. Sew F to the G sides of an F-G unit and add E to complete a white corner unit as shown in Figure 7; press seams toward F and then E.

Step 3. Join two H squares with two F-I units to complete a green corner unit as shown in Figure 8; press seams toward H and in one direction. Repeat to make two green corner units.

Figure 8

Step 4. Sew F to the G sides of a G-J unit and add E as shown in Figure 9 to make a blue corner unit; press seams toward F and then E.

Figure 9

Step 5. Arrange the corner units and join in rows referring to Figure 10; press seams toward green corner units. Join the rows to complete one block; press seams in one direction. Repeat to make four blocks.

Figure 10

COMPLETING THE BLUE SCHOOL GIRL'S PUZZLE BLOCKS

Step 1. Referring to Figure 11, sew G to I and F to G; press seams toward G.

Figure 11

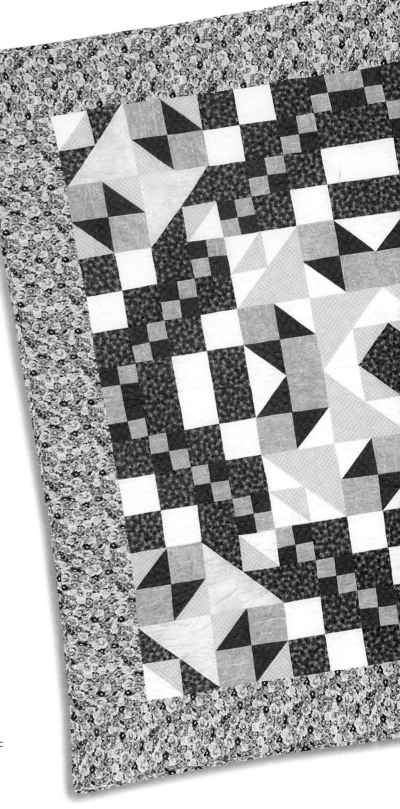

Step 2. To complete one block, sew J to the G sides of an F-G unit and add K to make a K corner unit as shown in Figure 12; press seams toward J and then K. Repeat to make two K corner units.

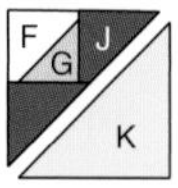

Make 8

Figure 12

Step 3. Sew H to the I side of a G-I unit as shown in Figure 13; repeat for four G-I-H units. Press seams toward H; repeat to make four units.

Figure 13

Step 4. Join two G-I-H units to make a G corner unit as shown in Figure 14; repeat to make two units. Press seams in one direction.

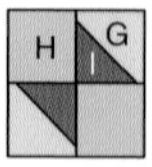

Figure 14

Step 5. Arrange and join the K corner units with the G corner units as shown in Figure 15; press seams toward K corner units and in one direction to complete one block. Repeat to make four blocks.

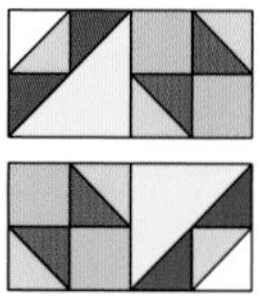

Figure 15

COMPLETING THE QUILT

Step 1. Referring to Figure 16, join two Blue School Girl's Puzzle blocks with two Carrie Nation blocks to make an X row; press seams toward Carrie Nation blocks. Repeat to make two X rows.

Step 2. Join two White School Girl's Puzzle blocks with two Carrie Nation blocks to make a Y row, again referring to Figure 16; press seams toward Carrie Nation blocks. Repeat to make two Y rows.

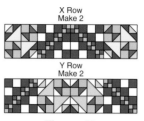

X Row
Make 2

Y Row
Make 2

Figure 16

Step 3. Arrange and join the X and Y rows referring to the Placement Diagram to complete the pieced center; press seams in one direction.

Step 4. Sew an L strip to opposite sides and M strips to the top and bottom of the pieced center to complete the top; press seams toward L and M strips.

Step 5. Complete the quilt using the previously cut binding strips and referring to Completing Your Quilt on page 170. ●

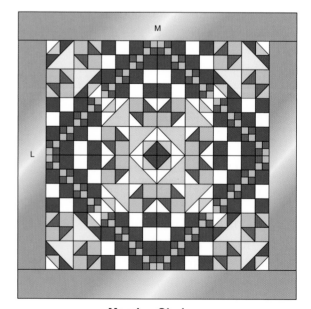

Morning Glorious
Placement Diagram
60" x 60"

Nine-Patch
6" x 6" Block
Make 32

Roman Stripe
6" x 6" Block
Make 32

Chained Nine-Patch

Nine-Patch and Roman Stripe blocks create the design in this easy-to-stitch quilt. The placement of the blocks results in a chain design, and the blocks get lost in the maze.

PROJECT SPECIFICATIONS

Skill Level: Intermediate
Quilt Size: 52" x 52"
Block Size: 6" x 6"
Number of Blocks: 64

MATERIALS

- ¼ yard red solid
- 2 yards peach tonal
- 2¼ yards floral
- Backing 58" x 58"
- Batting 58" x 58"
- All-purpose thread to match fabrics
- Quilting thread
- Basic sewing tools and supplies

CUTTING

Step 1. Cut three 6⅞" by fabric width strips floral; subcut strips into (16) 6⅞" squares. Cut each square in half on one diagonal to make 32 A triangles.

Step 2. Cut nine 2" by fabric width strips peach tonal for B pieces.

Step 3. Cut five 2¼" by fabric width strips peach tonal for D pieces.

Step 4. Cut seven 2" by fabric width strips floral for C pieces.

Step 5. Cut eight 2½" by fabric width E strips floral.

Step 6. Cut two 2½" by fabric width F strips red solid.

Step 7. Cut eight 2½" by fabric width G strips peach tonal.

Step 8. Cut five 2½" by fabric width strips peach tonal. Join strips on short ends to make one long strip; subcut strip into two 48½" H strips and two 52½" I strips.

Step 9. Cut six 2¼" by fabric width strips floral for binding.

PIECING THE ROMAN STRIPE BLOCKS

Step 1. Make 32 copies of the B/C/D paper-piecing pattern.

Step 2. Referring to Paper Piecing in the General Instructions and using one B/C/D paper-piecing pattern, pin one B strip on the unmarked side of the paper, covering the B area of the paper as shown in Figure 1.

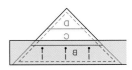

Figure 1

Step 3. Pin a C strip right sides together with the B strip; turn paper pattern over and stitch on the marked line between pieces B and C as shown in Figure 2.

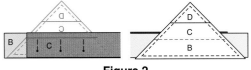

Figure 2

Step 4. Press C to the right side, trim strips, leaving roughly ¼" on each end as shown in Figure 3. *Note: The pieces will be trimmed exactly to the lines when all units are complete.*

Figure 3

Step 5. Pin a D strip right sides together with the stitched C strip as in Step 3, turn paper over and stitch on the line between pieces C and D.

Step 6. Press D to the right side and trim as in Step 4.

Step 7. Repeat Steps 1–5 with remaining paper foundations and strips to complete 32 B-C-D units.

Step 8. Trim all B-C-D units on the outside cutting line using a rotary cutter and ruler as shown in Figure 4.

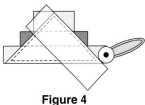

Figure 4

Step 9. Sew an A triangle to each B-C-D unit to complete one Roman Stripes block as shown in Figure 5; press seam toward A. Repeat to make 32 blocks.

Figure 5

COMPLETING THE NINE-PATCH BLOCKS

Step 1. Sew an F strip between two E strips to complete an E-F strip set; press seams toward E strip. Repeat for two strip sets.

Step 2. Subcut the E-F strip sets into (32) 2½" E-F units as shown in Figure 6.

Step 3. Sew an E strip between two G strips to complete an E-G strip set; press seams toward E. Repeat for four strip sets.

Step 4. Subcut the E-G strip sets into (64) 2½" E-G units, again referring to Figure 6.

Figure 6

Step 5. Sew one E-F unit between two E-G units to complete a Nine-Patch block as shown in

Figure 7; press seams toward the E-F unit. Repeat to make 32 blocks.

Figure 7

COMPLETING THE QUILT

Step 1. Join one Nine-Patch block and one Roman Stripe block to make a block unit as shown in Figure 8; press seam toward the Nine-Patch block. Repeat for two units.

Figure 8

Step 2. Join two block units as shown in Figure 9 to complete one chain unit; press seam in one direction. Repeat for 16 chain units.

Figure 9

Step 3. Join four chain units to make a row as shown in Figure 10; repeat for four rows. Press seams in adjoining rows in opposite directions.

Figure 10

Step 4. Join the rows to complete the pieced center referring to the Placement Diagram for positioning; press seams in one direction.

Step 5. Sew an H strip to opposite sides and I strips to the top and bottom of the pieced center; press seams toward H and I strips. Remove all paper patterns.

Step 6. Complete the quilt using the previously cut binding strips and referring to Completing Your Quilt on page 170. ●

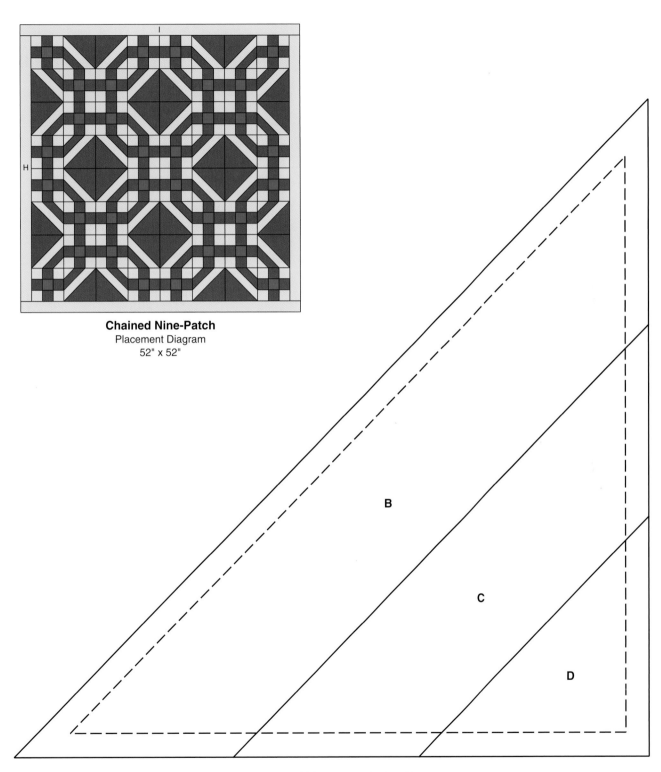

Chained Nine-Patch
Placement Diagram
52" x 52"

B

C

D

B/C/D Paper-Piecing Pattern
Make 32 copies

design by **LINDA MILLER**

 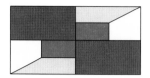 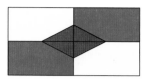 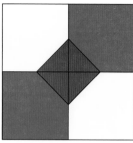

Four-Patch Variation
8" x 8" Block
Make 16

Stretched Four-Patch Variation
8" x 16" Block
Make 2

Stretched Bow Tie
8" x 16" Block
Make 4

Large Bow Tie
16" x 16" Block
Make 2

Different Twist

This quilt shares not only a variety of two blocks, but also a variety of size and shape of these two blocks. The Bow Tie blocks are made with either two large central squares or four large rectangles. This combination creates a skewed pathway down the diagonal of the quilt. The second block is a mitered Four-Patch Variation. Just by doubling the width of the square, a whole new illusion of that square is created. When the two are combined, the quilt takes on the appearance of many different squares.

PROJECT SPECIFICATIONS
Skill Level: Intermediate
Quilt Size: 64" x 64"
Block Sizes: 8" x 8", 8" x 16" and 16" x 16"
Number of Blocks: 24

MATERIALS
- ½ yard tan print
- ¾ yard red-with-black mottled
- ¾ yard red print
- 1 yard white print
- 1 yard black tonal
- 2¼ yards black-with-red print
- Backing 70" x 70"
- Batting 70" x 70"
- All-purpose thread to match fabrics
- Quilting thread
- Basic sewing tools and supplies

CUTTING

Step 1. Cut four 4½" by fabric width strips black tonal; subcut strips into (32) 4½" A squares.

Step 2. Cut two 4⅞" by fabric width strips each tan (B) and white (C) prints. Subcut strips into (32) 2½" rectangles each fabric.

Step 3. Cut each B rectangle at a 45-degree angle as shown in Figure 1; repeat with C rectangles, again referring to Figure 1.

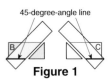

Figure 1

Step 4. Cut two 2½" by fabric width strips red-with-black mottled; subcut strips into (32) 2½" D squares.

Step 5. Cut four 4½" x 8½" E rectangles black tonal.

Step 6. Cut four 4½" x 4½" F squares white print. Measure up 2¹⁄₁₆" from the bottom right corner and make a mark as shown in Figure 2; measure over 4⅛" from the same corner and mark, again referring to Figure 2. Place a ruler

from mark to mark and remove corner to make an F piece, again referring to Figure 2; repeat to make four F pieces.

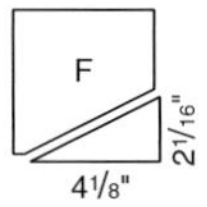

Figure 2

Step 7. Cut four 2½" x 4½" G rectangles red-with-black mottled.

Step 8. Cut four 2½" x 8½" rectangles tan print. Referring to Figure 3, measure, mark and trim off corner to make four H pieces.

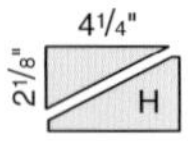

Figure 3

Step 9. Cut four 8½" x 8½" squares each red-with-black mottled (I) and white print (K).

Step 10. Cut one 4⅜" by fabric width strip black tonal; subcut strip into eight 4⅜" J squares.

Step 11. Prepare a template for L; cut as directed on the piece.

Step 12. Cut four 4½" x 8½" rectangles each white print (M) and red-with-black mottled (N). Referring to Figure 4, measure, mark and trim off corners to make two each M and N pieces.

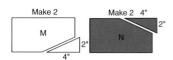

Figure 4

Step 13. Cut eight 1½" by fabric width strips black-with-red print. Join two strips on short ends to make one long O strip; press seams open. Repeat for four O strips.

Step 14. Cut eight 2½" by fabric width strips red print. Join two strips on short ends to make one long P strip; press seams open. Repeat for four P strips.

Step 15. Cut eight 5½" by fabric width strips black-with-red print. Join two strips on short ends

to make one long Q strip; press seams open. Repeat for four Q strips.

Step 16. Cut seven 2¼" by fabric width strips black-with-red print for binding.

PIECING THE LARGE BOW TIE BLOCKS

Step 1. Draw a diagonal line from corner to corner on the wrong side of each J square.

Step 2. To complete one Large Bow Tie block referring to Figure 5, place J on one corner of I and stitch on the marked line; trim seam to ¼". Press J to the right side to complete one I-J unit. Repeat for two units.

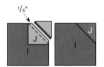
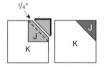

Figure 5   **Figure 6**

Step 3. Repeat Step 2 with J and K to complete two J-K units referring to Figure 6.

Step 4. Join the I-J and J-K units to complete one block as shown in Figure 7; press seams toward I-J units and in one direction. Repeat to make two blocks.

Figure 7

PIECING THE STRETCHED BOW TIE BLOCKS

Step 1. To piece one Stretched Bow Tie block, sew L to M as shown in Figure 8; press seam toward L. Repeat to make two L-M units.

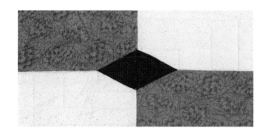

Step 2. Repeat Step 1 with LR and N, again referring to Figure 8. Repeat to make two LR-N units.

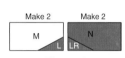
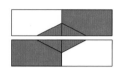

Figure 8   **Figure 9**

Step 3. Sew an L-M unit to an LR-N unit as shown in Figure 9; repeat. Press seams toward N pieces.

Step 4. Join the pieced units to complete one block; press seam in one direction. Repeat to make four blocks.

PIECING THE FOUR-PATCH VARIATION BLOCKS

Step 1. To complete one Four-Patch Variation block, sew B to D, starting at the outer edge and stitching to the angled edge of B, stopping stitching ¼" from angled edge as shown in Figure 10.

Figure 10   **Figure 11**

Step 2. Sew C to the B-D unit, starting at the outer edge and stopping stitching ¼" from the angled edge referring to Figure 11.

Step 3. Match and stitch the angled edges of B and C, pulling the D square upward and out of the way and stitching from the angled center to the outer edges of the pieces as shown in Figure 12; press seams away from D and toward B to complete one B-C-D unit. Repeat for two units.

Figure 12

Step 4. Sew A to a B-C-D unit as shown in Figure 13; repeat for two units. Press seams toward A.

Figure 13

Step 5. Join the two A units to complete one block; press seams in one direction. Repeat to make 16 blocks.

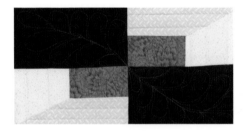

PIECING THE STRETCHED FOUR-PATCH VARIATION BLOCKS

Step 1. To complete one Stretched Four-Patch Variation block, sew H to G starting at the straight ends and stitching toward the angled edge of H, stopping stitching ¼" from end of G as shown in Figure 14.

Figure 14 **Figure 15**

Step 2. Repeat Step 1 with F to G as shown in Figure 15; press seam.
Step 3. Match and stitch the angled edges of F and H, pulling G upward and out of the way and stitching from the angled center to the outer

edges of the pieces as shown in Figure 16; press seams away from G and toward H to complete one block. Repeat to make four blocks.

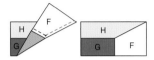

Figure 16

COMPLETING THE QUILT

Step 1. Arrange one of each type of block in rows to make a Bow Tie quarter as shown in Figure 17. Join the blocks to make rows; press seams in opposite directions.

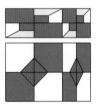

Figure 17

Step 2. Join the rows to complete one Bow Tie quarter; repeat for two Bow Tie quarters. Press seams in one direction.
Step 3. Arrange seven Four-Patch Variation blocks with one Stretched Bow Tie to make a Four-Patch quarter as shown in Figure 18. Join the blocks to make three rows; press seams in adjoining rows in opposite directions.

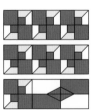

Figure 18

Step 4. Join the rows to complete one Four-Patch quarter; repeat for two Four-Patch quarters. Press seams in one direction.
Step 5. Arrange and join the quarter sections as shown in Figure 19 to complete the quilt center; press seams in opposite directions when

joining in rows and in one direction in the completed center.

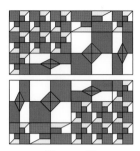

Figure 19

Step 6. Sew an O strip to a P strip to a Q strip with right sides together along the length to make a border strip; press seams toward P and Q strips. Repeat for four border strips.

Step 7. Center and sew a border strip to each side of the quilt center, stopping stitching ¼" from the end of ends of the quilt center as shown in Figure 20. Press seams toward border strips.

Figure 20

Step 8. Miter corner seams, matching seams of strips as shown in Figure 21. Trim mitered seams to ¼"; press seams open as shown in Figure 22 to complete the pieced top.

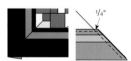

Figure 21   **Figure 22**

Step 9. Complete the quilt using the previously cut binding strips and referring to Completing Your Quilt on page 170. ●

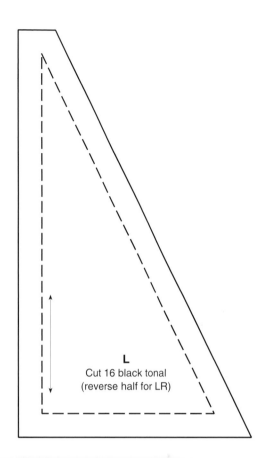

L
Cut 16 black tonal
(reverse half for LR)

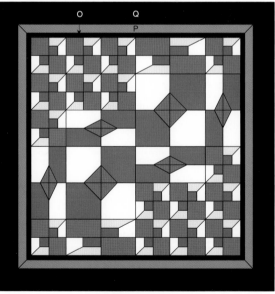

Different Twist
Placement Diagram
64" x 64"

design by **CONNIE KAUFFMAN**

Star Pathway
10½" x 10½" Block

Pathway to the Stars

When the Road to Tennessee block is overlaid with a simple Nine-Patch block, a whole new arrangement appears. Together, four blocks create a Pathway to the Stars.

PROJECT NOTE

Figure 1 shows how the Tennessee block is overlaid with a Nine-Patch block to create the new Star Pathway block used in this four-block quilt.

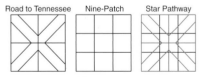

Figure 1

PROJECT SPECIFICATIONS

Skill Level: Beginner
Quilt Size: 33" x 33"
Block Size: 10½" x 10½"
Number of Blocks: 4

MATERIALS

- ¼ yard white mottled
- ¼ yard light green mottled
- ⅜ yard purple batik
- ½ yard textured light purple batik
- ⅝ yard dark green batik
- ¾ yard purple/green batik
- Backing 39" x 39"
- Batting 39" x 39"
- All-purpose thread to match fabrics
- Quilting thread
- Basic sewing tools and supplies

CUTTING

Step 1. Cut one 2¼" by fabric width strip textured light purple batik; subcut strip into (16) 2¼" A squares.

Step 2. Cut two 2¼" by fabric width strips white mottled; subcut strips into (32) 2¼" B squares.
Step 3. Cut one 4" by fabric width strip each purple (C) and purple/green (D) batiks; subcut strips into (16) 2¼" rectangles each for C and D.
Step 4. Cut two 2¼" by fabric width strips light green mottled; subcut strips into (32) 2¼" E squares.
Step 5. Cut two 4" by fabric width strips dark green batik; subcut strips into (16) 4" F squares.
Step 6. Cut four 2¼" x 21½" G strips textured light purple batik.
Step 7. Cut four 2¼" x 2¼" H squares purple batik.
Step 8. Cut four 4¾" x 25" I strips purple/green batik.
Step 9. Cut four 4¾" x 4¾" J squares purple batik.
Step 10. Cut four 2¼" by fabric width strips dark green batik.

COMPLETING THE BLOCKS

Step 1. Draw a diagonal line from corner to corner on the wrong side of each B and E square.
Step 2. Referring to Figure 2, place E right sides together on one corner of F; sew on the marked line. Trim seam to ¼"; press E to the right side.

Figure 2   **Figure 3**

Step 3. Repeat Step 2 with E on the opposite corner of F to complete an E-F unit as shown in Figure 3; repeat for 16 E-F units.
Step 4. Referring to Figure 4, sew B to C as in Step 2 to complete eight each B-C and reversed B-C units.

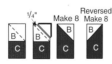

Figure 4

Step 5. Referring to Figure 5, sew B to D as in Step 2 to complete eight each B-D and reversed B-D units.

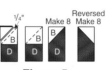

Figure 5   **Figure 6**

Step 6. To complete one block, sew B-C to E-F as shown in Figure 6; press seams toward E-F.
Step 7. Sew A to a B-D unit and sew to the B-C-E-F unit to complete one B-C-D corner unit as shown in Figure 7; press seams toward A and then E-F. Repeat to make two B-C-D corner units.

Figure 7   **Figure 8**

Step 8. Repeat Step 7 to complete one each B-C and B-D corner units as shown in Figure 8.
Step 9. Join one B-C-D corner unit and the B-C corner unit to complete half the block as shown

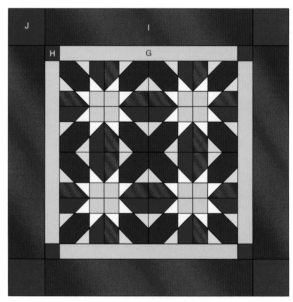

Pathway to the Stars
Placement Diagram
33" x 33"

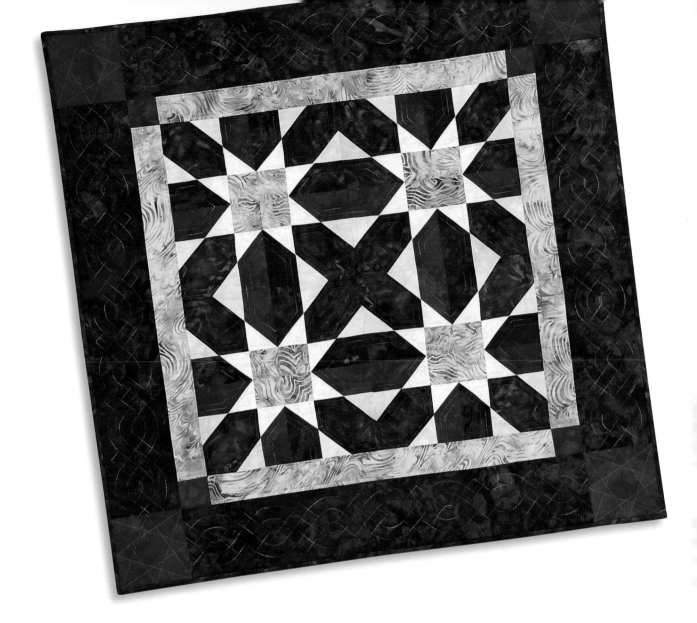

in Figure 9; press seam in one direction. Repeat to make a second half using the B-D corner unit, again referring to Figure 9. Join the halves to complete one block. Repeat to make four blocks.

Figure 9

COMPLETING THE QUILT

Step 1. Join two blocks to make a row; press seams in one direction. Repeat for two rows. Join the rows to complete the pieced center.

Step 2. Sew a G strip to opposite sides of the pieced center; press seams toward G.

Step 3. Sew H to each end of the remaining two G strips; press seams toward G.

Step 4. Sew a G-H strip to the remaining sides of the pieced center; press seams toward G-H strips.

Step 5. Sew an I strip to opposite sides of the pieced center; press seams toward I strips.

Step 6. Sew J to each end of the remaining two I strips; press seams toward I.

Step 7. Sew an I-J strip to the remaining sides of the pieced center to complete the top; press seams toward I-J strips.

Step 8. Complete the quilt using the previously cut binding strips and referring to Completing Your Quilt on page 170. ●

design by **MARIAN SHENK**

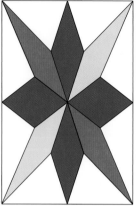

**Stretched
Eight-Pointed Star**
6" x 9" Block
Make 2

Stretched Starry Path
6" x 9" Block
Make 2

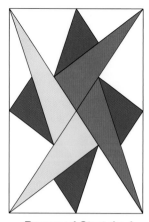

**Reversed Stretched
Starry Path**
6" x 9" Block
Make 2

**Reversed Stretched
Eight-Pointed Star**
6" x 9" Block
Make 2

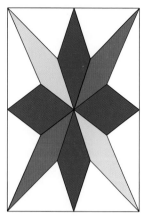

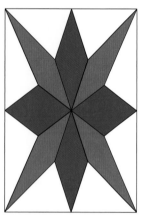

Stretched Center Star
6" x 9" Block
Make 1

Disoriented Dancing Stars

Stretch the Starry Path and Eight-Pointed Star designs from squares to rectangles to create star blocks that seem to dance across the quilt. Stitch the stretched blocks using red, white and blue fabrics for a patriotic look, or change the colors for a seasonal wall quilt.

PROJECT SPECIFICATIONS

Skill Level: Advanced
Quilt Size: 27" x 36"
Block Size: 6" x 9"
Number of Blocks: 9

MATERIALS

- ⅓ yard light blue tonal
- ¾ yard white silver metallic
- ⅞ yard red mottled
- ⅞ yard dark blue tonal
- Backing 33" x 42"
- Batting 33" x 42"
- All-purpose thread to match fabrics
- Quilting thread
- Template material
- Basic sewing tools and supplies

CUTTING

Step 1. Prepare templates using pattern pieces given; cut as directed on each piece.
Step 2. Cut two 2" x 27½" M strips and two 2" x 18½" N strips red mottled.
Step 3. Cut four 2" x 2" O squares light blue tonal.
Step 4. Cut two 3½" x 30½" P strips and two 3½" x 27½" Q strips dark blue tonal.
Step 5. Cut four 2¼" by fabric width strips red mottled for binding.

PIECING THE STRETCHED EIGHT-POINTED STAR BLOCKS

Step 1. To complete one Stretched Eight-Pointed Star block, sew E between a red mottled D and a light blue tonal DR, stopping stitching at the dot at the end of the seam allowance as shown in Figure 1; press seams in one direction. Repeat for two D-E units.

Figure 1

Step 2. Join the two D-E units with C pieces as shown in Figure 2, stopping stitching at the dot at the end of the seam allowance. Press seams in one direction.

Figure 2

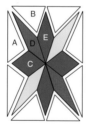

Figure 3

Step 3. Set in A and B pieces referring to Figure 3 to complete one block; press seams toward A and B pieces. Repeat to make two blocks.
Step 4. Repeat to make two Reversed

Eight-Pointed Star blocks referring to the block drawing for positioning of the D and DR pieces.

PIECING THE STRETCHED STARRY PATH BLOCKS

Step 1. To complete one Stretched Starry Path block, sew J to H to K as shown in Figure 4; press seams in one direction. Repeat to make two J-H-K units.

Figure 4

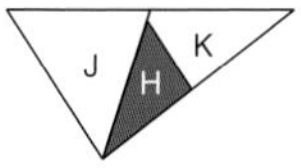

Figure 5

Step 2. Add a red mottled G to the H side of one J-H-K unit and a light blue mottled G to the remaining unit referring to Figure 5; press seams toward G.

Step 3. Sew I to HR to L as shown in Figure 6; press seams in one direction. Repeat to make two I-HR-L units.

Figure 6

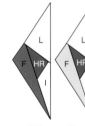
Figure 7

Step 4. Sew a red mottled F to the HR side of one I-HR-L unit and a light blue mottled F to the remaining unit referring to Figure 7; press seams toward F.

Step 5. Join the pieced sections to make two diagonal half-blocks as shown in Figure 8; press seams toward F.

Figure 8

Step 6. Join the diagonal half-blocks to complete one block; press seam in one direction. Repeat to make two blocks.

Step 7. Repeat to make two Reversed Stretched Starry Path blocks referring to the block drawing for positioning of the F pieces.

PIECING THE STRETCHED CENTER STAR BLOCK

Step 1. Complete one Stretched Center Star Block referring to Steps 1–3 for the Stretched Eight-Pointed Star blocks, except use all red mottled D and DR pieces.

COMPLETING THE QUILT

Step 1. Sew a Stretched Starry Path block between a Stretched Eight-Pointed Star block and a Reversed Stretched Eight-Pointed Star block to make an X row referring to the Placement Diagram for positioning; press seams toward the center block.

Step 2. Sew the Stretched Center Star block between the Reversed Stretched Starry Path blocks to make a Y row referring to the Placement Diagram for positioning; press seams away from the center block.

Step 3. Join the X and Y rows referring to the Placement Diagram to complete the pieced center; press seams in one direction.

Step 4. Sew an M strip to opposite long sides of the pieced center; press seams toward M.

Step 5. Sew an O square to each end of each N strip; press seams toward N. Sew an N-O strip to the top and bottom of the pieced center; press seams toward N-O strips.

Step 6. Sew the P strips to opposite long sides and Q strips to the top and bottom of the pieced center; press seams toward P and Q to complete the quilt top.

Step 7. Complete the quilt using the previously cut binding strips and referring to Completing Your Quilt on page 170. ●

B
Cut 20 white silver metallic
(reverse half for BR)

C
Cut 10 dark blue tonal

A
Cut 20 white silver metallic
(reverse half for AR)

Disoriented Dancing Stars
Placement Diagram
27" x 36"

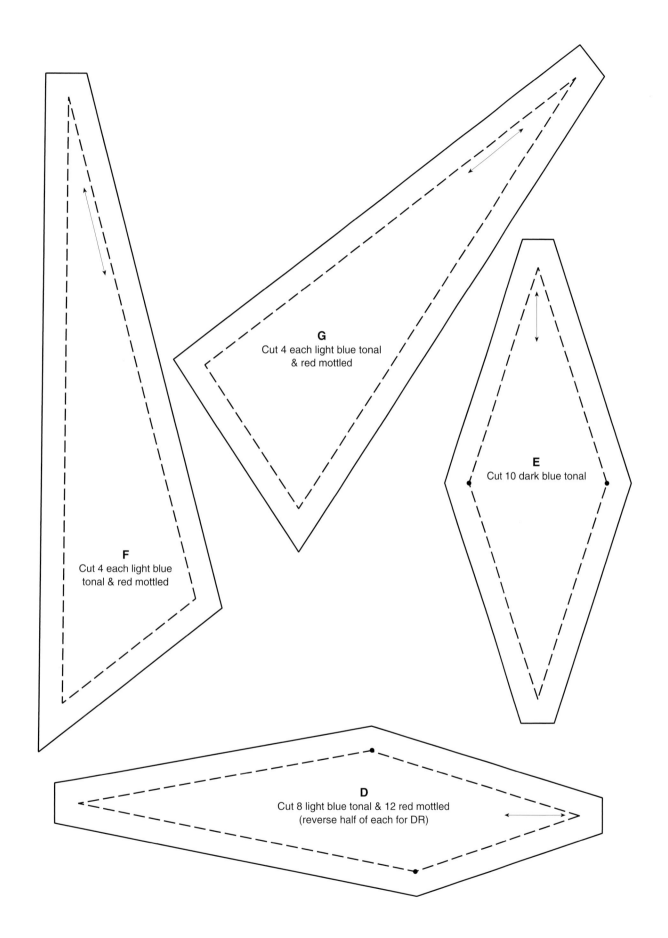

G
Cut 4 each light blue tonal
& red mottled

E
Cut 10 dark blue tonal

F
Cut 4 each light blue
tonal & red mottled

D
Cut 8 light blue tonal & 12 red mottled
(reverse half of each for DR)

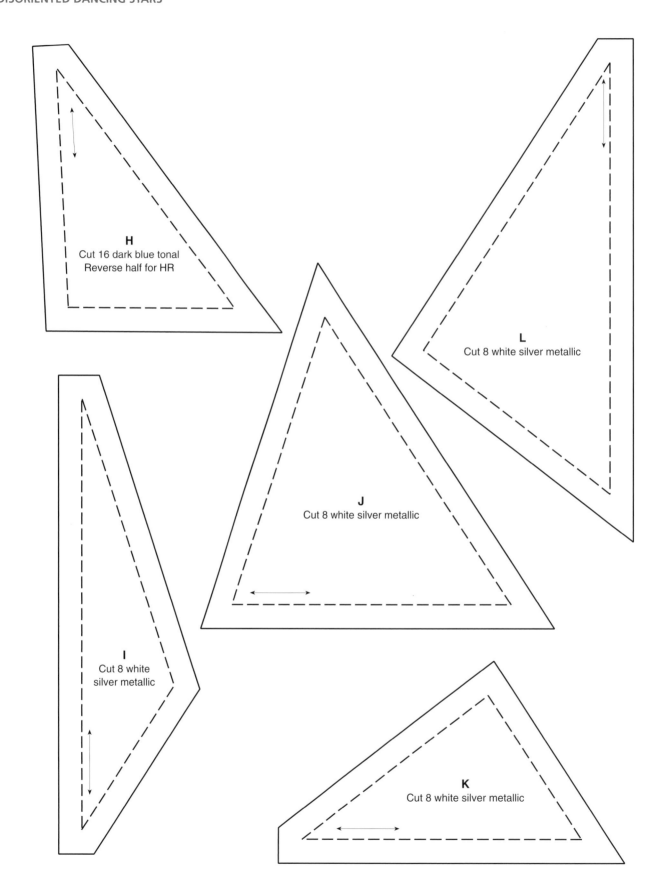

H
Cut 16 dark blue tonal
Reverse half for HR

L
Cut 8 white silver metallic

J
Cut 8 white silver metallic

I
Cut 8 white
silver metallic

K
Cut 8 white silver metallic

Elongated Cups & Saucers
9" x 15" Block
Make 5

Elongated Snowball
9" x 15" Block
Make 4

Piney Woods

The traditional Snowball and Cups & Saucers blocks are elongated to change their appearance. This simple stretch creates this unusual design. The fabrics add the cabin-decor look.

PROJECT NOTES

Figure 1 shows the classic Snowball and Cups & Saucers blocks. In the quilt shown, the Snowball block edges align perfectly with the Flying Geese units in the Cups & Saucers blocks making it hard to tell where one block ends and the other begins. Because the Flying Geese units require angled pieces, these units are paper-pieced.

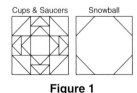

Figure 1

PROJECT SPECIFICATIONS

Skill Level: Advanced Beginner
Quilt Size: 43½" x 57"
Block Size: 9" x 15"
Number of Blocks: 9

MATERIALS

- ⅛ yard each 4 coordinating green tonals or mottleds
- ⅝ yard medium green mottled
- 1½ yards brown tonal
- 1½ yards brown print
- 1⅝ yards tan print
- Backing 50" x 63"
- Batting 50" x 63"
- All-purpose thread to match fabrics
- Quilting thread
- Basic sewing tools and supplies

CUTTING

Step 1. Make 10 copies of each A/B and A/C paper-piecing patterns.

Step 2. Cut (10) 2½" by fabric width strips tan print for A.

Step 3. Cut (20) 3½" x 3½" assorted B squares

from the coordinating green fabrics and medium green mottled.

Step 4. Cut (20) 2¼" x 5½" assorted C rectangles from the coordinating green fabrics and medium green mottled.

Step 5. Cut five 3½" x 5½" D rectangles tan print.

Step 6. Cut four 9½" x 15½" G rectangles tan print.

Step 7. Cut two 4½" x 45½" H and two 2½" x 31½" J strips along the length of the brown tonal.

Step 8. Cut two 4¾" x 45½" I strips and two 4½" x 31½" K strips along the length of the brown print.

Step 9. Cut four 2½" x 2½" L squares brown tonal; mark a diagonal line from corner to corner on the wrong side of each square.

Step 10. Cut four 6¾" x 6½" M pieces brown print.

Step 11. Prepare template for E/F using pattern given. Cut as directed on the piece.

Step 12. Cut six 2¼" by fabric width strips medium green mottled for binding.

PIECING THE ELONGATED CUPS & SAUCERS BLOCKS

Step 1. Referring to Paper Piecing in the General Instructions, fold an A/B pattern along the lines between pieces to make creases. Pin a B square to the unmarked side of the creased A/B pattern.

Step 2. Pin an A strip right sides together with the B square along the creased line between pieces 1 and 2, leaving a ¼" seam allowance beyond the line; turn paper over and stitch on the 1-2 line as shown in Figure 2.

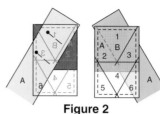 

Figure 2   **Figure 3**

Step 3. Turn the stitched unit over and press A to the right side as shown in Figure 3.

Step 4. Turn the stitched unit over again and trim the A strip to extend barely beyond outside marked line of the pattern as shown in Figure 4.

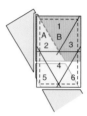

Figure 4

Step 5. Repeat with the A strip in the #3 position as shown in Figure 5.

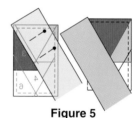

Figure 5

Step 6. Continue adding pieces to the paper foundation in numerical order until the paper is covered. Trim fabric even with outside pattern line of the A-B unit. Repeat to make 10 A-B units as shown in Figure 6.

Figure 6

Step 7. Repeat Steps 1–4 to make 10 A-C units, again referring to Figure 6.

Step 8. Sew E to F to complete an E-F unit as shown in Figure 7; press seam toward F. Repeat with ER and FR to make a reversed E-F unit. Repeat to make 10 each E-F and reversed E-F units.

Figure 7

Step 9. Join an E-F and reversed E-F unit with an A-B unit to make the top row as shown in Figure 8; repeat for the bottom row. Press seams away from the A-B units.

Figure 8

Step 10. Join two A-C units with D to make the center row as shown in Figure 9; press seams toward D.

Figure 9

Step 11. Join the rows as shown in Figure 10 to complete one Elongated Cups & Saucers block; press seams toward the center row. Repeat to make five blocks.

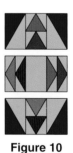

Figure 10

COMPLETING THE ELONGATED SNOWBALL BLOCKS

Step 1. Mark 3⅛" in from each corner on each 9½" end of G as shown in Figure 11.

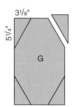

Figure 11

Step 2. Mark 5¼" down from each corner on each 15½" side of G, again referring to Figure 11.

Step 3. Connect the marks at each corner and cut along the marked lines, again referring to Figure 11.

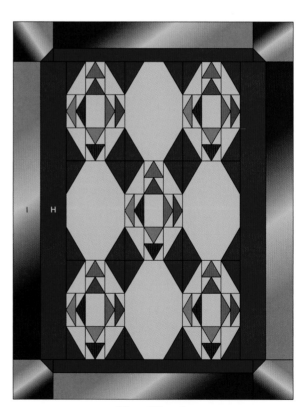

Piney Woods
Placement Diagram
43½" x 57"

Step 4. Sew an F or FR triangle to the corners of G referring to Figure 12 to complete one Elongated Snowball block; press seams toward F and FR. Repeat to make four blocks.

Figure 12

COMPLETING THE QUILT

Step 1. Sew one Elongated Snowball block between two Elongated Cups & Saucers blocks to make a row referring to the Placement Diagram; press seams toward the center block. Repeat for two rows.

Step 2. Sew an Elongated Cups & Saucers block between two Elongated Snowball blocks to make the center row, again referring to the Placement Diagram; press seams away from the center block.

Step 3. Join the rows referring to the Placement Diagram to complete the pieced center; press seams in one direction.

Step 4. Sew a J strip to a K strip with right sides together along the length; press seams toward K. Repeat for two J-K strips.

Step 5. Sew an H strip to an I strip with right sides together along the length; press seams toward I. Repeat for two H-I strips.

Step 6. Referring to Figure 13, place an L square on one corner of M; stitch on the marked line. Trim seam to ¼"; press L to the right side to complete an L-M unit. Repeat for four L-M units.

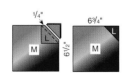

Figure 13

Step 7. Sew an H-I strip to opposite long sides of the pieced center; press seams toward H-I strips.

Step 8. Sew an L-M unit to each end of each J-K strip as shown in Figure 14; press seams toward J-K strips.

Figure 14

Step 9. Sew the J-K-L-M strips to the top and bottom of the pieced center to complete the top; press seams toward the pieced strips.

Step 10. Remove all paper patterns.

Step 11. Complete the quilt using the previously cut binding strips and referring to Completing Your Quilt on page 170. ●

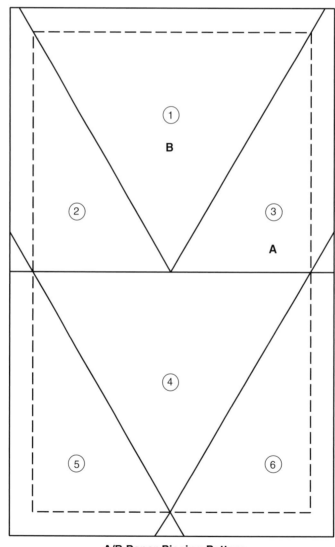

A/B Paper-Piecing Pattern
Make 10 copies

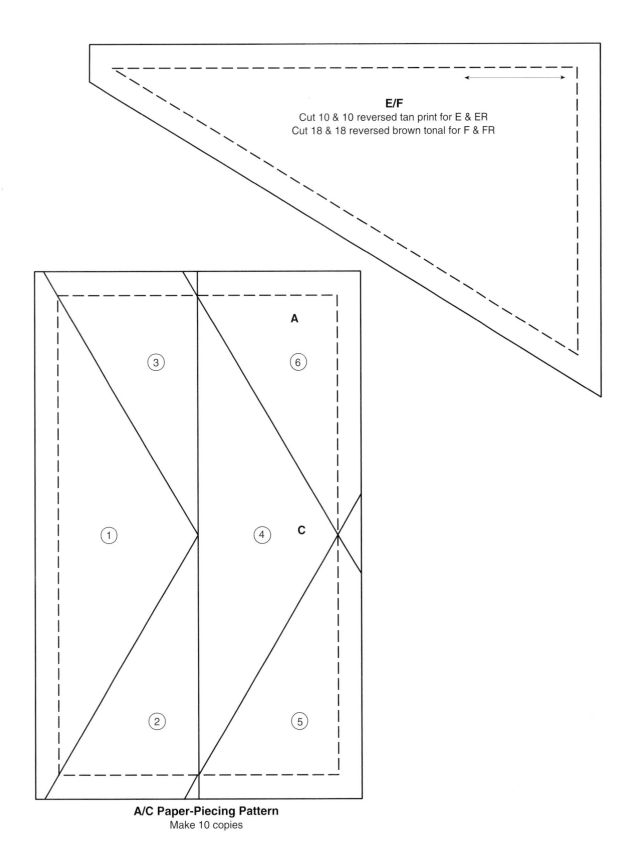

E/F
Cut 10 & 10 reversed tan print for E & ER
Cut 18 & 18 reversed brown tonal for F & FR

A

③

⑥

①

④ C

②

⑤

A/C Paper-Piecing Pattern
Make 10 copies

design by **MARIAN SHENK**

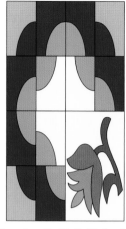

Drunkard's Path Tulip A1
10" x 18" Block
Make 2

Drunkard's Path Tulip A2
10" x 18" Block
Make 2

Drunkard's Path Tulip Garden

Using rectangles instead of squares to create Drunkard's Path units changes the movement created by the curved pieces. Add four stretched Tulip appliqué designs, and you have a garden with a curved path around it.

PROJECT SPECIFICATIONS

Skill Level: Advanced
Quilt Size: 28" x 44"
Block Size: 10" x 18"
Number of Blocks: 4

MATERIALS

- Scraps pink, dark pink and green fabrics
  for appliqué
- ¼ yard light green solid
- ½ yard dark green print
- ½ yard gold print
- ½ yard cream tonal
- ½ yard rose tonal
- Backing 31" x 50"
- Batting 31" x 50"
- All-purpose thread to match fabrics
- Quilting thread
- Template material
- ½ yard lightweight fusible web
- 1 package green wide bias binding
- Water-erasable marker or pencil
- Basic sewing tools and supplies

CUTTING

Step 1. Cut four 5½" x 9½" rectangles cream tonal for A1 and A2 rectangles; fold and crease each rectangle to mark the centers.

Step 2. Prepare templates for appliqué shapes using patterns given. Trace shapes onto the paper side of the lightweight fusible web as directed on shapes for number to cut.

Step 3. Cut out shapes, leaving a margin around each shape.

Step 4. Fuse shapes onto the wrong side of the fabric scraps and gold print as directed on patterns for color; cut out shapes on traced lines. Remove paper backing.

Step 5. Cut one 5" by fabric width strip each cream tonal (B) and light green solid (D); subcut strips into (12) 3" rectangles each fabric for B and C.

Step 6. Cut two 5" by fabric width strips dark green print; subcut strips into (24) 3" D rectangles.

Step 7. Prepare template for E/F using pattern given; cut as directed on the piece.

Step 8. Cut two 2" x 20½" G strips and two 2" x 39½" H strips gold print.

Step 9. Cut two 3" x 39½" I strips and two 3" x 28½" J strips rose tonal.

COMPLETING THE BLOCKS

Step 1. Using a water-erasable marker or pencil, transfer full-size tulip design to A1 and A2 rectangles using creased lines and center mark on pattern for centering to make two each A1 and A2 designs as shown in Figure 1.

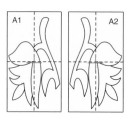

Figure 1

Step 2. Arrange appliqué shapes on A1 and A2 on marked lines in numerical order; fuse shapes in place.

Step 3. Using thread to match fabric, machine satin-stitch around shapes in numerical order to complete the appliquéd A1 and A2 units.

Step 4. Trim the E/F template along the B/C/D trimming line as shown in Figure 2.

Figure 2

Step 5. Lay the trimmed template on each B, C and D rectangle, matching the outside straight edges referring to Figure 3; mark along the curved edge of the template.

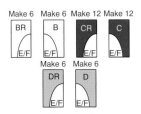

Figure 3

Step 6. Trim each B, C and D piece along the marked line.

Step 7. Sew E and ER to B and C and F and FR to D as shown in Figure 4; press seams toward E, ER, F and FR pieces.

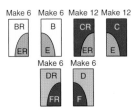

Figure 4

Step 8. To make one Drunkard's Path Tulip A1 block, arrange the pieced units in rows with an A1 unit referring to Figure 5.

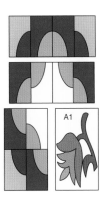

Figure 5

Step 9. Join units in rows as arranged; press seams in adjoining rows in opposite directions. Join the rows to complete the block; press seams in one direction. Repeat for two A1 blocks.

Step 10. To make one Drunkard's Path Tulip A2 block, repeat Steps 8 and 9 with A2 units referring to Figure 6. Repeat for two A2 blocks.

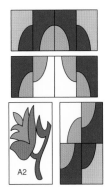

Figure 6

COMPLETING THE QUILT

Step 1. Join an A1 and A2 block to make a row referring to the Placement Diagram for positioning of blocks; press seam in one direction. Repeat for two rows.

Step 2. Join the rows to complete the pieced center; press seams in one direction.

Step 3. Sew G strips to the top and bottom of the pieced center; press seams toward G.

Step 4. Sew an H strip to an I strip with right sides together along length; press seams toward I. Repeat for two H-I strips.

Step 5. Sew an H-I strip to opposite long sides of the pieced center; press seams toward H-I strips.

Step 6. Sew a J strip to the top and bottom of the pieced center; press seams toward J to complete the top.

Step 7. Complete the quilt using purchased green wide bias binding and referring to Completing Your Quilt on page 170. ●

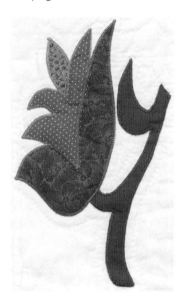

Drunkard's Path Tulip Garden
Placement Diagram
28" x 44"

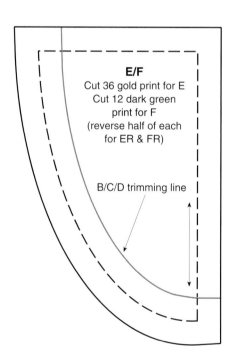

E/F
Cut 36 gold print for E
Cut 12 dark green
print for F
(reverse half of each
for ER & FR)

B/C/D trimming line

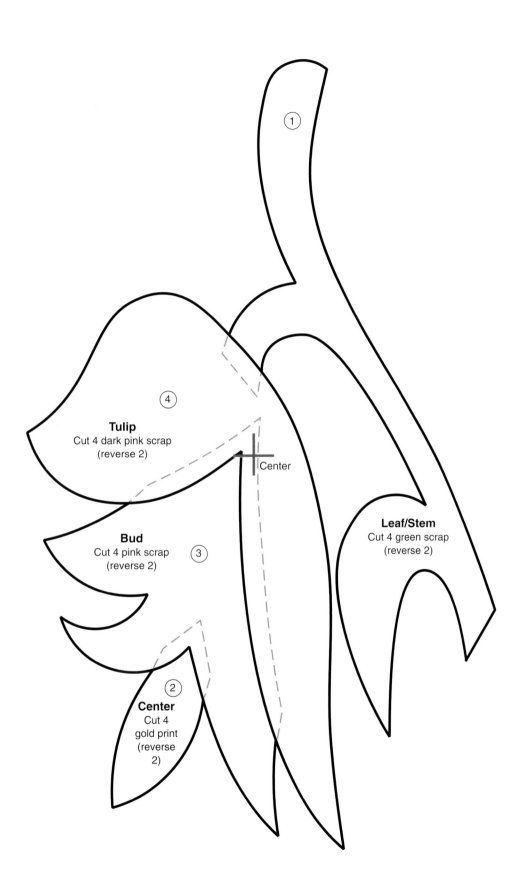

Tulip
Cut 4 dark pink scrap
(reverse 2)

Bud
Cut 4 pink scrap
(reverse 2)

Leaf/Stem
Cut 4 green scrap
(reverse 2)

Center

Center
Cut 4
gold print
(reverse
2)

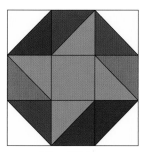

Blue Ribbon
9" x 9" Block

Blue Ribbon Twist

The twisting pattern of a ribbon is achieved with the use of

a single block and a random assortment of dark blue fabrics.

Lighter blue in the center makes the center star design stand out.

PROJECT SPECIFICATIONS
Skill Level: Beginner
Quilt Size: 48" x 48"
Block Size: 9" x 9"
Number of Blocks: 16

MATERIALS
- ⅛ yard each 8 different navy tonals
- ⅜ yard each 4 different medium blue tonals
- ⅞ yard navy print
- ⅞ yard cream-with-blue print
- Backing 54" x 54"
- Batting 54" x 54"
- All-purpose thread to match fabrics
- Quilting thread
- Basic sewing tools and supplies

CUTTING
Step 1. Cut one 3½" by fabric width strip from each of the four medium blue tonals; subcut each strip into four 3½" A squares. Trim the remainder of each strip to 2½" and set aside for binding.

Step 2. Cut one 3⅞" by fabric width strip from each of the four medium blue tonals; subcut each strip into eight 3⅞" squares. Cut each square in half on one diagonal to make 16 B triangles of each fabric.

Step 3. Cut one 3⅞" by fabric width strip from each navy tonal; subcut each strip into eight 3⅞" squares. Cut each square in half on one diagonal to make 128 C triangles.

Step 4. Cut four 3⅞" by fabric width strips cream-with-blue print; subcut strips into (32) 3⅞"

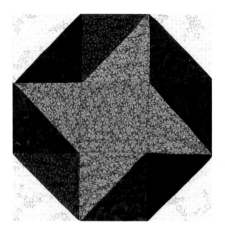

squares. Cut each square in half on one diagonal to make 64 D triangles.

Step 5. Cut two 2" x 36½" E strips and two 2" x 39½" F strips cream-with-blue print.

Step 6. Cut two 5" x 39½" G strips navy print.

Step 7. Cut three 5" by fabric width strips navy print. Join strips on short ends to make one long strip; press seams open. Subcut strip into two 48½" H strips.

Step 8. Cut one 2½" strip each from three medium blue tonals; cut strips in half to make six 21"–22" strips. Set aside five strips for binding and one strip for another project.

PIECING THE BLOCKS

Step 1. Sew B to C to complete a B-C unit as shown in Figure 1; press seam toward C. Repeat to make 64 B-C units.

Figure 1

Step 2. Sew C to D to complete a C-D unit, again referring to Figure 1; press seam toward C. Repeat to make 64 C-D units.

Step 3. To complete one block, sew a B-C unit to opposite sides of A to make the block center row referring to Figure 2; press seams toward A.

Figure 2

Step 4. Sew a C-D unit to opposite sides of a B-C unit to make the top row as shown in Figure 3; press seams toward C-D units. Repeat for bottom row.

Figure 3

Step 5. Join the rows as shown in Figure 4 to complete one block; press seams toward the center row. Repeat to make 16 blocks.

Figure 4

COMPLETING THE QUILT

Step 1. Join four blocks to make a row; press seams in one direction. Repeat for four rows.

Step 2. Join the rows to complete the pieced center; press seams in one direction.

Step 3. Sew an E strip to the top and bottom and F strips to opposite sides of the pieced center; press seams toward E and F strips.

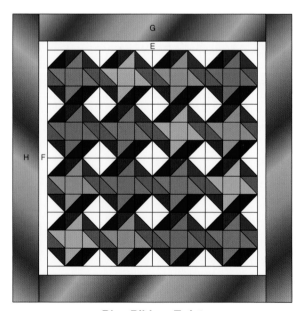

Blue Ribbon Twist
Placement Diagram
48" x 48"

Step 4. Sew a G strip to the top and bottom and H strips to opposite sides of the pieced center; press seams toward G and H strips to complete the pieced top.

Step 5. Complete the quilt using the previously cut 2½"-wide binding strips and referring to Completing Your Quilt on page 170. ●

design by **JOHANNA WILSON**

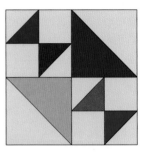

Summer Fox & Geese
8" x 8" Block
Make 12

Autumn Fox & Geese
8" x 8" Block
Make 4

Changing Seasons

The Fox & Geese pattern stands alone in the borders, but four of the blocks join in the center to create a medallion. When framed, the center creates a seasonal transition from the colors of autumn to summer.

PROJECT SPECIFICATIONS
Skill Level: Beginner
Quilt Size: 45" x 45"
Block Size: 8" x 8"
Number of Blocks: 16

MATERIALS
- ½ yard brown print
- ½ yard cream/green check
- ⅝ yard total medium-to-dark greens
- 1 yard gold tonal
- 1⅛ yards floral
- Backing 51" x 51"
- Batting 51" x 51"
- All-purpose thread to match fabrics
- Quilting thread
- Basic sewing tools and supplies

CUTTING
Step 1. Cut two 4⅞" by fabric width strips gold tonal; subcut strips into (16) 4⅞" squares. Cut each square on one diagonal to make 32 A triangles.
Step 2. Cut one 6½" by fabric width strip floral; subcut strip into two 6½" squares. Cut each square in half on one diagonal to make four L triangles.
Step 3. Trim the remainder of the 6½"-wide strip to 4⅞"; subcut strip into four 4⅞" squares. Cut each square in half on one diagonal to make eight B triangles.

Step 4. Cut one 2⅞" by fabric width strip floral; subcut strip into eight 2⅞" squares. Cut each square in half on one diagonal to make 16 C triangles.

Step 5. Cut three 2⅞" by fabric width strips gold tonal; subcut strips into (32) 2⅞" squares. Cut each square in half on one diagonal to make 64 D triangles.

Step 6. Cut four 2½" by fabric width strips gold tonal; subcut strips into (64) 2½" E squares.

Step 7. Cut two 12¼" x 12¼" squares brown print; cut each square on one diagonal to make four F triangles.

Step 8. Cut (12) 4⅞" x 4⅞" squares medium-to-dark greens; cut each square in half on one diagonal to make 24 G triangles.

Step 9. Cut (24) 2⅞" x 2⅞" squares medium-to-dark greens; cut each square in half on one diagonal to make 48 H triangles.

Step 10. Cut two 12½" x 12½" squares cream/green check; cut each square on both diagonals to make eight I triangles.

Step 11. Cut two 6½" x 6½" squares cream/green check; cut each square in half on one diagonal to make four J triangles.

Step 12. Cut one 12½" by fabric width strip floral; subcut strip into three 12½" squares. Cut each square on both diagonals to make 12 K triangles.

Step 13. Cut five 2¼" by fabric width strips floral for binding.

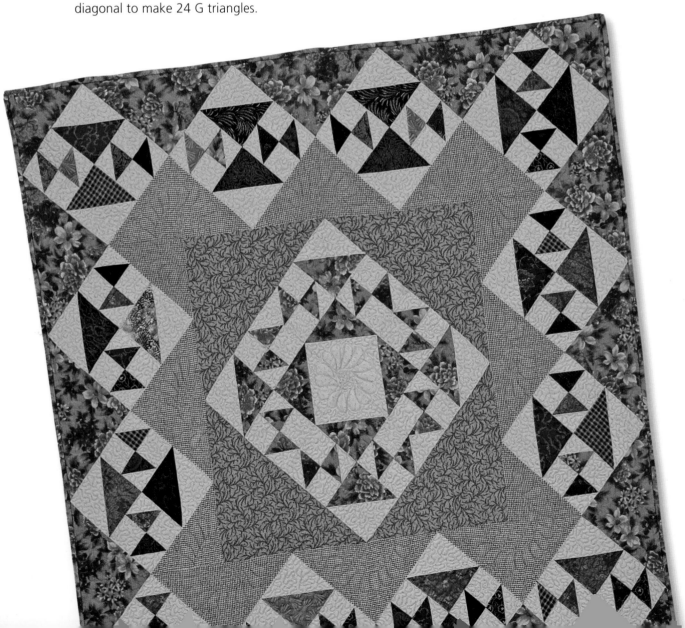

PIECING THE AUTUMN
FOX & GEESE BLOCKS

Step 1. Sew A to B along the diagonal to make an A-B unit as shown in Figure 1; repeat for eight A-B units. Press seams toward B.

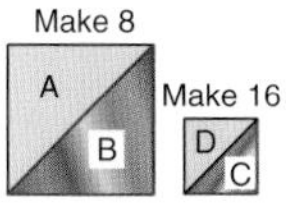

Make 8

Make 16

Figure 1

Step 2. Sew C to D along the diagonal to make a C-D unit, again referring to Figure 1; repeat for 16 C-D units. Press seams toward C.

Step 3. To complete one block, sew E to a C-D unit as shown in Figure 2; press seam toward E. Repeat for four C-D-E units.

Figure 2

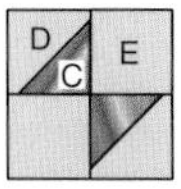

Figure 3

Step 4. Join two C-D-E units as shown in Figure 3; press seam in one direction. Repeat for two joined units.

Step 5. Sew a joined C-D-E unit with an A-B unit to make a row as shown in Figure 4; press seam toward the A-B unit. Repeat for two rows.

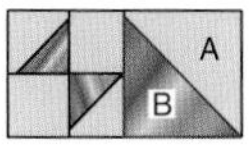

Figure 4

Step 6. Join the two rows to complete one Autumn Fox & Geese block as shown in Figure 5; press seam in one direction. Repeat to make four blocks.

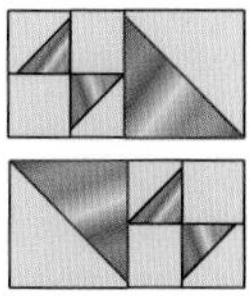

Figure 5

COMPLETING THE SUMMER
FOX & GEESE BLOCKS

Step 1. Referring to Figure 6, sew D to H; repeat for 48 D-H units. Press seams toward H.

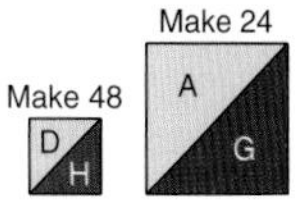

Make 24

Make 48

Figure 6

Step 2. Again referring to Figure 6, sew A to G; repeat for 24 A-G units. Press seams toward G.

Step 3. To complete one Summer Fox & Geese block, sew E to D-H as shown in Figure 7; repeat for two units. Press seams toward E.

Figure 7

Step 4. Join the two E-D-H units referring to Figure 8; press seam in one direction. Repeat for two joined units.

Figure 8

Step 5. Sew a joined E-D-H unit with an A-G unit as shown in Figure 9 to make a row; press seam toward A-B unit; repeat for two rows.

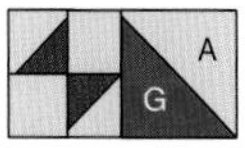

Figure 9

Step 6. Join the rows to complete one Summer Fox & Geese block referring to Figure 10; press seam in one direction. Repeat to make 12 blocks.

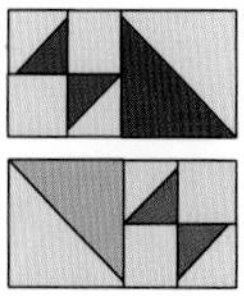

Figure 10

COMPLETING THE QUILT

Step 1. Join four Autumn Fox & Geese blocks to make the quilt center as shown in Figure 11; press seams in one direction.

Figure 11

Step 2. Sew F to each side of the quilt center as shown in Figure 12; press seams toward F.

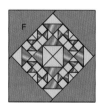

Figure 12

Step 3. Join two Summer Fox & Geese blocks with one each I and K triangles and two J triangles to make an end unit as shown in Figure 13; press seams away from the blocks and in one direction. Repeat to make two end units.

Figure 13

Step 4. Sew an end unit to opposite sides of the quilt center; press seams toward end units.

Step 5. Join two Summer Fox & Geese blocks with one K triangle and three I triangles to make a side unit as shown in Figure 14; press seams away from blocks and in one direction. Repeat to make two side units.

Figure 14

Step 6. Sew a side unit to the remaining sides of the quilt center; press seams toward side units.

Step 7. Join one Summer Fox & Geese block with one L and two K triangles to make a corner unit as shown in Figure 15; press seams away from the block. Repeat to make four corner units.

Figure 15

Step 8. Sew a corner unit to each corner of the quilt center to complete the top; press seams toward corner units.

Step 9. Complete the quilt using the previously cut binding strips and referring to Completing Your Quilt on page 170. ●

Changing Seasons
Placement Diagram
45" x 45"

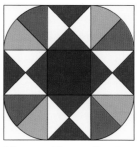

Mystery Flower Garden
9" x 9" Block
Make 13

Nine-Patch Variation
9" x 9" Block
Make 12

Autumn Garden

A simple Nine-Patch design takes on elements of the Mystery Flower Garden block to create confusion when trying to figure out where one block ends and the other begins.

PROJECT SPECIFICATIONS

Skill Level: Intermediate
Quilt Size: 55" x 55"
Block Size: 9" x 9"
Number of Blocks: 25

MATERIALS

- 31 (1½" x 22") B strips red prints, mottleds or tonals
- 38 (1½" x 22") A strips green prints, mottleds or tonals
- 13 (3½" x 3½") F squares assorted brown prints
- ½ yard burgundy print
- ½ yard gold print
- ½ yard green mottled
- 1⅔ yards burgundy tonal
- 1⅔ yards cream solid
- Backing 61" x 61"
- Batting 61" x 61"
- All-purpose thread to match fabrics
- Quilting thread
- Basic sewing tools and supplies

CUTTING

Step 1. Cut four 3⅞" by fabric width strips cream solid; subcut strips into (34) 3⅞" squares. Cut each square in half on one diagonal to make 68 C triangles.

Step 2. Cut two 2½" x 51½" J strips and two 2½" x 55½" K strips along the length of the burgundy tonal.

Step 3. Cut seven 4¼" by remaining fabric width strips burgundy tonal; subcut strips into (43) 4¼" D squares.

Step 4. Cut five 4¼" by fabric width strips cream solid; subcut strips into (43) 4¼" E squares.

Step 5. Prepare templates for G/H and I using patterns given; cut as directed on each piece.

Step 6. Cut six 2¼" by fabric width strips burgundy print for binding.

PIECING THE NINE-PATCH VARIATION BLOCKS

Step 1. Sew a B strip between two A strips with right sides together along length to make an A strip set; repeat for 15 A strip sets. Press seams toward B.

Step 2. Sew an A strip between two B strips with right sides together along length to make a B strip set; repeat for eight B strip sets. Press seams toward B.

Step 3. Subcut the A strip sets into (208) 1½" A units and the B strips into (104) 1½" B units as shown in Figure 1.

Figure 1

Step 4. Sew a B unit between two A units to complete an A-B unit as shown in Figure 2; press seams in one direction. Repeat for 104 A-B units; set aside 44 units for border and side units.

Figure 2

Step 5. Draw a diagonal line from corner to corner on each E square.

Step 6. Referring to Figure 3, layer an E square on a D square; sew ¼" on each side of the drawn line. Cut apart on the drawn line. Repeat for all D and E squares to complete 86 D-E units.

Figure 3

Step 7. Cut each of the D-E units in half on one diagonal to make 86 each smaller D-E and reversed D-E units as shown in Figure 4. Set aside 38 smaller D-E units and 66 reversed D-E units for Mystery Flower Garden blocks.

Figure 4

Step 8. Join one smaller D-E unit with C as shown in Figure 5 to make a C unit; repeat to make 48 C and 20 reversed C units, again referring to Figure 5. Set aside the reversed C units for border units.

Figure 5

Step 9. To complete one Nine-Patch Variation block, sew a C unit to opposite sides of an A-B unit to make the center row as shown in Figure 6; press seams toward the C units.

Figure 6

Step 10. Sew an A-B unit to opposite sides of a C unit as shown in Figure 7 to make the bottom row; repeat to make the top row. Press seams toward the C units.

Figure 7

Step 11. Join the rows referring to Figure 8 to complete one block; press seams in one direction. Repeat to make 12 blocks.

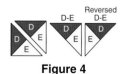

Figure 8

PIECING THE MYSTERY FLOWER GARDEN BLOCKS

Step 1. Join two smaller D-E units to complete a side unit as shown in Figure 9; repeat for 19 side units.

Step 2. Join two reversed D-E units to make a side unit, again referring to Figure 9; repeat for 33 side units to total 52 side units. ***Note:*** *From*

this point, there are no reversed units. Before these were stitched together, the units themselves were reversed.

Make 19   Make 33

Figure 9

Step 3. Referring to Figure 10, sew G to H to make a G-H unit; repeat for 52 units. Press seams toward G.

Figure 10   **Figure 11**

Step 4. Sew I to the G-H units, matching the center of I to the seam between the pieces to complete 52 corner units as shown in Figure 11; press seams toward I.

Step 5. To complete one Mystery Flower Garden block, sew a side unit to opposite sides of F to complete the center row as shown in Figure 12; press seams toward F.

Make 2

Make 1

Figure 12

Step 6. Sew a corner unit to opposite sides of a side unit to make a row, again referring to Figure 12; press seams toward side units. Repeat for two rows.

Step 7. Sew the rows to the top and bottom of the center row to complete one block as shown in Figure 13; press seams in one direction. Repeat for 13 blocks.

Figure 13

COMPLETING THE QUILT

Step 1. Sew an A-B unit to opposite sides of each reversed C unit to make border units as shown in Figure 14; press seams toward reversed C units.

Figure 14

Step 2. Referring to Figure 15, join three Mystery Flower Garden blocks with two Nine-Patch Variation blocks and two border units to make an X row; press seams toward the Nine-Patch Variation blocks and border units. Repeat for three X rows.

Step 3. Again referring to Figure 15, join three Nine-Patch Variation blocks with two Mystery

Flower Garden blocks and two border units to make a Y row; press seams toward the Nine-Patch Variation blocks. Repeat for two Y rows.

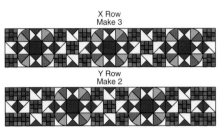

X Row
Make 3

Y Row
Make 2

Figure 15

Step 4. Join the X and Y rows, beginning and ending with an X row referring to the Placement Diagram; press seams in one direction.

Step 5. Join five border units to make a strip as shown in Figure 16; repeat to make two strips. Add an A-B unit to each end of each strip; press seams in one direction.

Figure 16

Autumn Garden
Placement Diagram
55" x 55"

Step 6. Sew the strips to the top and bottom of the pieced center; press seams toward pieced strips.

Step 7. Sew a J strip to opposite sides and the K strips to the remaining sides of the pieced center to complete the quilt top; press seams toward strips.

Step 8. Complete the quilt using the previously cut binding strips and referring to Completing Your Quilt on page 170. ●

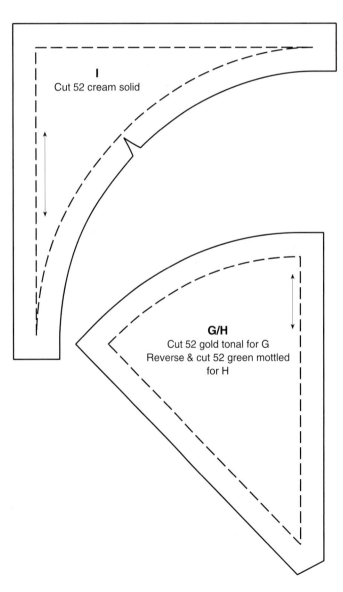

I
Cut 52 cream solid

G/H
Cut 52 gold tonal for G
Reverse & cut 52 green mottled
for H

design by **JULIE WEAVER**

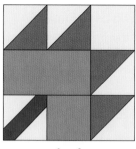

Leaf
6" x 6" Block
Make 10

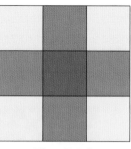

Nine-Patch
6" x 6" Block
Make 3

Bountiful Harvest

The combination of the Leaf and Nine-Patch blocks crisscrosses the center of this large table runner or wall banner. The addition of sashing strips gives the illusion of looking through a garden lattice.

PROJECT SPECIFICATIONS
Skill Level: Beginner
Quilt Size: 55¼" x 25¼"
Block Size: 6" x 6"
Number of Blocks: 13

MATERIALS
- ⅛ yard brown print
- ⅜ yard red print 1
- ½ yard red print 2
- ½ yard tan print
- ¾ yard green print
- 1¼ yards floral
- Backing 61 x 31"
- Batting 61" x 31"

- All-purpose thread to match fabrics
- Quilting thread
- Basic sewing tools and supplies

CUTTING
Step 1. Cut four 2½" by fabric width strips red print 1; subcut two strips into (10) 2½" A squares and (10) 4½" B rectangles. Cut the remaining strips in half to make four 20"–22" A strips; set aside one half-strip for another project.
Step 2. Cut two 2⅞" by fabric width strips each tan print (C) and red print 2 (D); subcut strips into (20) 2⅞" squares each fabric for C and D.
Step 3. Cut one 2½" by fabric width strip each brown (E) and tan (H) prints; subcut strips into

(10) 2½" squares each fabric for E and H.

Step 4. Cut one 2" by fabric width strip tan print; subcut strip into (20) 2" F squares.

Step 5. Cut one 2½" by fabric width strip each tan print (H) and red print 2 (G); cut each strip in half to make two 20"–22" strips each fabric. Set aside one G half-strip for another project.

Step 6. Cut one 1½" by fabric width strip red print 2; subcut strip into (24) 1½" I squares.

Step 7. Cut six 1½" by fabric width strips green print; subcut strips into (36) 6½" J pieces.

Step 8. Cut two 11¼" x 11¼" squares floral; cut each square in half on both diagonals to make eight K triangles.

Step 9. Cut two 11½" x 11½" squares floral; cut each square in half on one diagonal to make four L triangles.

Step 10. Cut three 2½" by fabric width strips green print. Join strips on short ends to make one long strip; press seams open. Subcut strip into two 2½" x 51¼" M strips.

Step 11. Cut two 2½" x 25¾" N strips green print.

Step 12. Cut five 2¼" by fabric width strips floral for binding.

PIECING THE LEAF BLOCKS

Step 1. Draw a diagonal line from corner to corner on the wrong side of each C and F square.

Step 2. Place a C square right sides together with D. Referring to Figure 1, stitch ¼" on each side of the marked line.

Figure 1

Figure 2

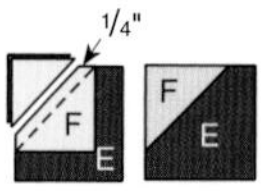

Step 3. Cut apart on the marked line to make two C-D units; press seams toward D. Repeat for 40 units.

Step 4. Referring to Figure 2, place an F square right sides together with E; stitch on the marked line. Trim seam to ¼" and press F to the right side.

Step 5. Repeat Step 4 on the opposite corner of E as shown in Figure 3 to complete an E-F unit. Repeat for 10 E-F units.

Figure 3

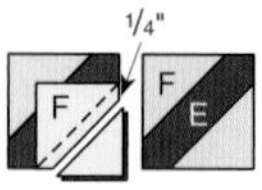

Figure 4

Step 6. To complete one block, sew a C-D unit to one side and an E-F unit to the opposite side of A as shown in Figure 4; press seams toward A.

Step 7. Sew a C-D unit to B as shown in Figure 5; press seam toward B.

Figure 5

Figure 6

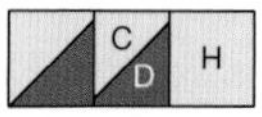

Step 8. Join two C-D units with H as shown in Figure 6; press seam toward H.

Step 9. Join the pieced units as shown in Figure 7 to complete one Leaf block; press seams in one direction. Repeat to make 10 blocks.

Figure 7

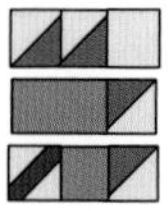

PIECING THE NINE-PATCH BLOCKS

Step 1. Sew an A strip between two H strips with right sides together along length; press seams toward A. Subcut strip sets into six 2½" A-H units as shown in Figure 8.

Figure 8

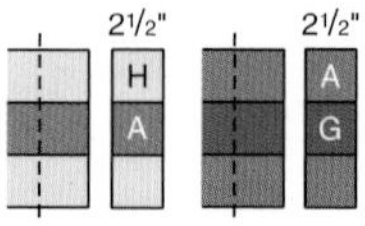

Step 2. Sew a G strip between two A strips with right sides together along length; press seams toward A. Subcut strip set into three 2½" A-G units, again referring to Figure 8.

Step 3. Sew an A-G unit between two A-H units to complete one Nine-Patch block as shown in

Figure 9; press seams toward A-G units. Repeat to make three blocks.

Figure 9

COMPLETING THE QUILT

Step 1. Arrange and join the pieced blocks with the I, J, K and L pieces in diagonal rows as shown in Figure 10; press seams toward J in the I-J rows and toward J in the block rows.

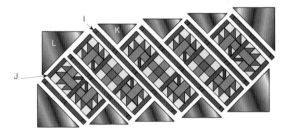

Figure 10

Step 2. Join the block and I-J rows to complete the pieced center; press seams toward the I-J rows.

Step 3. Sew an M strip to opposite long sides and N strips to the short ends of the pieced center; press seams toward M and N strips to complete the pieced top.

Step 4. Complete the quilt using the previously cut binding strips and referring to Completing Your Quilt on page 170. ●

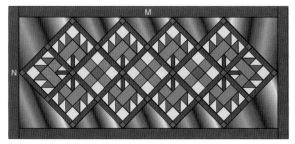

Bountiful Harvest
Placement Diagram
55¼" x 25¼"

design by **JULIE WEAVER**

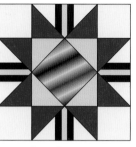

Star Crossed
9" x 9" Block
Make 2

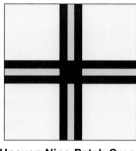

Uneven Nine-Patch Cross
9" x 9" Block
Make 1

Autumn Song Table Runner

Two Star Crossed blocks and an Uneven Nine-Patch Cross block get together to form the basis for this autumn runner. Setting the three blocks with sashing creates a woven flow from one star to the other.

PROJECT NOTE

Pay special attention to the fabric cuts when making this runner. Some creative math was used to make the star blocks finish at 9".

PROJECT SPECIFICATIONS

Skill Level: Beginner
Quilt Size: 40" x 20"
Block Size: 9" x 9"
Number of Blocks: 3

MATERIALS

- ¼ yard gold print
- ⅓ yard green print
- ⅜ yard red check
- ½ yard cream print
- 1 yard burgundy floral
- Backing 46" x 26"
- Batting 46" x 26"
- All-purpose thread to match fabrics
- Quilting thread
- Basic sewing tools and supplies

CUTTING

Step 1. Cut two 5" x 5" A squares burgundy floral.

Step 2. Cut one 2¾" by fabric width strip each gold (B) and cream (D) prints; subcut each strip into eight 2¾" squares each for B and D.

Step 3. Cut two 2¾" by fabric width strips red

check; subcut strips into (16) 2¾" C squares.

Step 4. Cut two 2" by fabric width E strips cream print.

Step 5. Cut four 1" by fabric width strips green print for F and H.

Step 6. Cut two 1" by fabric width strips gold print for G and I.

Step 7. Cut one 4¼" by fabric width strip cream print; subcut strip into four 4¼" J squares.

Step 8. Cut one 2" x 2" K square green print.

Step 9. Cut three 1½" by fabric width strips green print; subcut strips into (10) 9½" L strips.

Step 10. Cut one 1½" by fabric width strip gold print; subcut strip into eight 1½" M squares.

Step 11. Cut three 1½" by fabric width strips red check; cut two of the strips into two 31½" N strips and the remaining strip into two 13½" O strips.

Step 12. Cut three 4" by fabric width strips burgundy floral; subcut two of the strips into two 33½" P strips and the remaining strip into two 20½" Q strips.

Step 13. Cut four 2¼" by fabric width strips burgundy floral for binding.

COMPLETING THE STAR CROSSED BLOCKS

Step 1. Draw a diagonal line from corner to corner on the wrong side of each B square.

Step 2. Referring to Figure 1, sew a B square to one corner of A on the marked line; trim seam to ¼" and press B to the right side. Repeat on each corner of B to complete an A-B unit. Repeat for two A-B units.

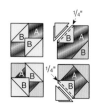

Figure 1

Step 3. Sew a G strip between two F strips with right sides together along length; add an E strip

to each long edge to make a strip set. Press seams toward F.

Step 4. Subcut the E-F-G strip set into eight 2¾" E-F-G units as shown in Figure 2.

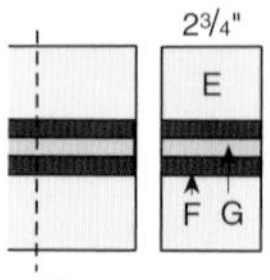

Figure 2

Step 5. Draw a diagonal line from corner to corner on the wrong side of each C square.

Step 6. Referring to Figure 3, place a C square right sides together on an E-F-G unit; stitch on the drawn line. Trim seam to ¼" and press C to the right side.

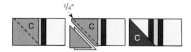

Figure 3

Step 7. Repeat on the remaining end of the E-F-G unit to complete a side unit as shown in Figure 4; repeat to make eight side units.

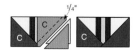

Figure 4

Step 8. To complete one Star Crossed block, sew a side unit to opposite sides of the A-B unit to complete the center row as shown in Figure 5; press seams toward A-B.

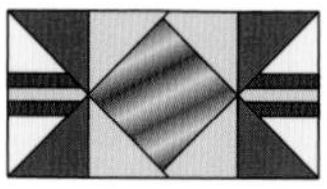

Figure 5    **Figure 6**

Step 9. Sew a D square to each end of two side units to complete the top row as shown in Figure 6; press seams toward D. Repeat to make the bottom row.

Step 10. Sew the top and bottom rows to the center row as shown in Figure 7 to complete one block; press seams in one direction. Repeat to make two blocks.

Figure 7

COMPLETING THE UNEVEN NINE-PATCH CROSS BLOCK

Step 1. Sew an I strip between two H strips with right sides together along length to make an H-I strip set; press seams toward H strips.

Step 2. Subcut the H-I strip set into four 4¼" units as shown in Figure 8.

Figure 8

Step 3. To complete one Uneven Nine-Patch Cross block, join two H-I units with K to make the center row as shown in Figure 9; press seams toward K.

Figure 9

Step 4. Join two J squares with an H-I unit to make the top row as shown in Figure 10; press

seams toward J. Repeat to make the bottom row.

Figure 10

Step 5. Sew the center row between the top and bottom rows to complete the block as shown in Figure 11; press seams away from the center row.

Figure 11

COMPLETING THE QUILT

Step 1. Join the Uneven Nine-Patch Cross block with the Star Crossed Blocks and four L strips as shown in Figure 12; press seams toward L.

Figure 12

Step 2. Join four M squares with three L strips to make an L-M row as shown in Figure 13; press seams toward L.

Figure 13

Step 3. Sew an L-M strip to opposite long sides of the pieced block row to complete the pieced center; press seams toward L-M strips.

Step 4. Sew an N strip to opposite long sides and the O strips to the short ends of the pieced center; press seams toward N and O strips.

Step 5. Sew a P strip to opposite long sides and the Q strips to the short ends of the pieced center to complete the runner top; press seams toward Q and P.

Step 6. Complete the quilt using the previously cut binding strips and referring to Completing Your Quilt on page 170. ●

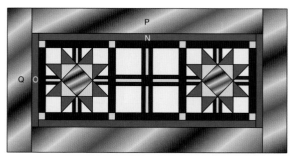

Autumn Song Table Runner
Placement Diagram
40" x 20"

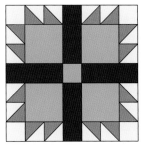

Bear Paw
7" x 7" Block
Make 12

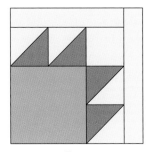

Paw
7" x 7" Block
Make 4

Garden of the Bear

Four large "paws" are joined to form the center of this autumnal wall hanging. The Bear Paw block that is created in the center is surrounded by 12 small "bears." Use of the same sashing fabric throughout provides interest and continuity.

PROJECT SPECIFICATIONS

Skill Level: Beginner
Quilt Size: 52" x 52"
Block Size: 7" x 7"
Number of Blocks: 16

MATERIALS

- ⅝ yard rust tonal
- ¾ yard gold tonal
- ¾ yard cream tonal
- 1⅛ yards green print
- 1¼ yards dark green tonal
- Backing 58" x 58"
- Batting 58" x 58"
- All-purpose thread to match fabrics
- Quilting thread
- Basic sewing tools and supplies

CUTTING

Step 1. Cut three 2½" by fabric width strips gold tonal; subcut strips into (48) 2½" A squares.

Step 2. Cut one 4½" by fabric width strip gold tonal; subcut strip into eight 4½" G squares.

Step 3. Cut two 2½" by fabric width strips gold tonal; subcut strips into (25) 2½" N squares.

Step 4. Cut eight 2" x 2" O squares gold tonal.

Step 5. Cut five 1⅞" by fabric width strips each

rust (B) and cream (C) tonals; subcut strips into (96) 1⅞" squares each fabric for B and C.

Step 6. Cut two 1½" by fabric width strips cream tonal; subcut strips into (48) 1½" D squares.

Step 7. Cut one 2½" by fabric width strip cream tonal; subcut strip into four 2½" J squares.

Step 8. Cut one 2⅞" by fabric width strip cream tonal; subcut strip into eight 2⅞" I squares.

Step 9. Cut two 1½" by fabric width strips cream tonal; subcut strips into four 6½" K strips and four 7½" L strips.

Step 10. Cut two 3½" by fabric width strips dark green tonal; subcut strips into (48) 1½" E strips.

Step 11. Cut nine 2" by fabric width strips dark green tonal; cut four of these strips into 38½" P strips. Join the remaining strips on short ends to make one long strip; press seams open. Subcut the strip into four 49½" R strips.

Step 12. Cut six 2¼" by fabric width strips dark green tonal for binding.

Step 13. Cut one 1½" by fabric width strip rust tonal; subcut strip into (12) 1½" F squares.

Step 14. Cut one 2⅞" by fabric width strip rust tonal; subcut the strip into eight 2⅞" H squares.

Step 15. Cut eight 2½" by fabric width strips green print; subcut strips into (40) 7½" M strips.

Step 16. Cut four 4½" x 41½" Q strips green print.

PIECING THE BEAR PAW BLOCKS

Step 1. Draw a diagonal line from corner to corner on all C squares.

Step 2. Referring to Figure 1, place a C square right sides together with B; stitch ¼" on each side of the marked line. Cut apart on the marked line; press open with seam toward B to make two B-C units. Repeat with all B and C squares to make 192 B-C units.

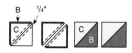

Figure 1

Step 3. To complete one Bear Paw block, join two B-C units as shown in Figure 2; repeat to make four joined units and four reversed joined units. Press seams toward B.

Figure 2

Step 4. Sew one joined B-C unit to A as shown in Figure 3; press seam toward A.

Figure 3

Step 5. Sew D to the B end of a reversed joined B-C unit as shown in Figure 4; press seam toward D.

Figure 4

Step 6. Sew the B-C-D unit to the adjacent side of the A-B-C unit as shown in Figure 5 to complete one Bear Paw unit; press seams toward the B-C-D unit. Repeat to make four Bear Paw units.

Figure 5

Step 7. Join two Bear Paw units with E to make a row as shown in Figure 6; repeat. Press seams toward E.

Figure 6

Step 8. Join two E pieces with F as shown in Figure 7; press seams toward F.

Figure 7

Step 9. Sew the E-F unit between the two rows as shown in Figure 8 to complete one Bear Paw

block; press seams toward the E-F unit. Repeat to make 12 blocks.

Figure 8

COMPLETING THE PAW BLOCKS

Step 1. Mark a diagonal line from corner to corner on the wrong side of the I triangles.

Step 2. Referring to Figure 9, place an I square right sides together with H; stitch ¼" on each side of the marked line. Cut apart on the marked line; press open with seam toward H to make two H-I units. Repeat with all H and I squares to make 16 H-I units.

Figure 9

Step 3. To complete one Paw block, join two H-I units to make a joined H-I unit as shown in Figure 10; repeat for a reversed joined unit. Press seams toward H.

Figure 10

Step 4. Sew a joined H-I unit to G as shown in Figure 11; press seam toward G.

Figure 11

Step 5. Sew J to the H end of a reversed joined H-I unit as shown in Figure 12; press seam toward J.

Figure 12

Step 6. Sew the H-I-J unit to the G-H-I unit as shown in Figure 13; press seam toward the H-I-J unit.

Figure 13

Step 7. Sew K to one I side and L to the adjacent I side of the pieced unit as shown in Figure 14 to complete one Paw block; press seams toward K and L. Repeat to make four Paw blocks.

Figure 14

COMPLETING THE QUILT

Step 1. Join four Bear Paw blocks with five M strips to make the top row as shown in Figure 15; press seams toward M strips. Repeat to make the bottom row.

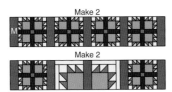

Figure 15

Step 2. Join two Bear Paw blocks with two Paw blocks and five M strips to make a center row, again referring to Figure 15; press seams toward M strips. Repeat to make two center rows.

Step 3. Join four M strips with five N squares to make a sashing row as shown in Figure 16; press seams toward M. Repeat to make five sashing rows.

Figure 16

Step 4. Join the block rows with the sashing rows to complete the pieced center referring to the Placement Diagram for positioning of rows; press seams toward sashing rows.

Step 5. Sew a P strip to opposite sides of the pieced center; press seams toward P strips.

Step 6. Sew an O square to each end of each remaining P strip; press seams toward P. Sew an O-P strip to the remaining sides of the pieced center; press seams toward O-P strips.

Step 7. Sew a Q strip to opposite sides of the pieced center; press seams toward Q strips.

Step 8. Sew a G square to each end of each remaining Q strip; press seams toward Q. Sew the G-Q strips to the remaining sides of the pieced center; press seams toward G-Q strips.

Step 9. Sew an R strip to opposite sides of the pieced center; press seams toward R strips.

Step 10. Sew an O square to each end of each remaining R strip; press seams toward R. Sew the O-R strips to the remaining sides of the pieced center; press seams toward O-R strips.

Step 11. Complete the quilt using the previously cut binding strips and referring to Completing Your Quilt on page 170. ●

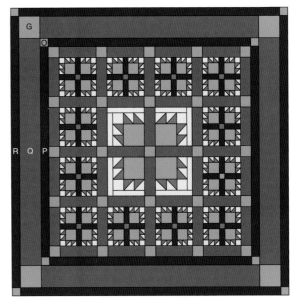

Garden of the Bear
Placement Diagram
52" x 52"

design by **JUDITH SANDSTROM**

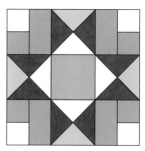

Ohio Star
18" x 18" Block
Make 5

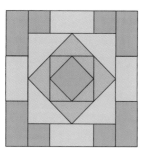

Framed Square
18" x 18" Block
Make 4

Southwest Stars

The color variations on the corners and outer edges of the Ohio Star block provide an interesting background and allow the stars to be connected to the Framed Square blocks for an overall Southwest flavor.

PROJECT SPECIFICATIONS

Skill Level: Beginner
Quilt Size: 60" x 60"
Block Size: 18" x 18"
Number of Blocks: 9

MATERIALS

- ⅝ yard black print
- ⅝ yard cream tonal
- 1¼ yards blue print
- 1⅓ yards rust tonal
- 1⅝ yards tan tonal
- Backing 66" x 66"
- Batting 66" x 66"
- All-purpose thread to match fabrics
- Quilting thread
- Basic sewing tools and supplies

CUTTING

Step 1. Cut one 6½" by fabric width strip rust tonal; subcut strip into five 6½" A squares.

Step 2. Cut eight 3½" by fabric width strips rust tonal; subcut three strips into (28) 3½" squares. Set aside four squares for N. Draw a diagonal line from corner to corner on the wrong side of each remaining square for I. Join the remaining five strips on short ends to make a long strip; press seams open. Subcut the strip into eight 24½" M strips.

Step 3. Cut one 5⅛" by fabric width strip rust

tonal; subcut strip into eight 5⅛" squares. Cut each square on one diagonal to make 16 J triangles.

Step 4. Cut two 3½" by fabric width E strips cream tonal.

Step 5. Cut one 7¼" by fabric width strip each cream (B) and tan (D) tonals: subcut each strip into five 7¼" squares. Cut each square on both diagonals to make 20 each B and D triangles.

Step 6. Cut two 7¼" by fabric width strips black print; subcut strips into (10) 7¼" squares. Cut each square on both diagonals to make 40 C triangles.

Step 7. Cut four 3½" by fabric width F strips blue print; set aside two strips for E-F units. Subcut two strips into (16) 3½" F squares.

Step 8. Cut four 6½" by fabric width strips blue print; subcut three strips into (36) 3½" G pieces. Subcut the remaining strip into four 6½" H squares.

Step 9. Cut two 6½" by fabric width strips tan tonal; subcut strips into (20) 3½" L pieces.

Step 10. Cut two 6⅞" by fabric width strips tan tonal; subcut strips into eight 6⅞" squares. Cut each square in half on one diagonal to make 16 K triangles.

Step 11. Cut seven 2¼" by fabric width strips tan tonal for binding.

PIECING THE OHIO STAR BLOCKS

Step 1. To complete one Ohio Star block, sew C to D; press seam toward C. Sew C to B; press seam toward C.

Step 2. Join the C-D and B-C units as shown in Figure 1 to complete a side unit; press seams in one direction. Repeat to make four side units.

Figure 1

Figure 2

Step 3. Sew E to F with right sides together along the length to make an E-F strip set; repeat to make two strip sets. Press seam toward F. Subcut the strip sets into (20) 3½" E-F units as shown in Figure 2.

Step 4. Sew an E-F unit to G to complete a corner unit as shown in Figure 3; press seam toward G. Repeat to make four corner units.

Figure 3

Figure 4

Step 5. Sew a side unit to opposite sides of A to make the center row as shown in Figure 4; press seams toward A.

Step 6. Sew a side unit between two corner units to complete the top row, again referring to Figure 4; press seams toward the corner units. Repeat to make the bottom row.

Step 7. Sew the top and bottom rows to the center row to complete one Ohio Star block referring to the block drawing; press seams toward the center row. Repeat to make five blocks.

COMPLETING THE FRAMED SQUARE BLOCKS

Step 1. To complete one Framed Square block,

place I right sides together on one corner of H referring to Figure 5; stitch on the marked line. Trim seam to ¼"; press I to the right side. Repeat on all sides of H to complete the H-I unit, again referring to Figure 5.

Figure 5

Step 2. Sew J to each side of the H-I unit as shown in Figure 6; press seams toward J. Sew K to each side of this unit to complete the block center, again referring to Figure 6; press seams toward K.

Figure 6   **Figure 7**

Step 3. Sew F to each end of L to make a side unit; press seams toward F. Repeat to make two side units.

Step 4. Sew a side unit to opposite sides of the block center as shown in Figure 7; press seams toward the side units.

Step 5. Sew L between two G pieces to complete a G side unit; press seams toward G. Repeat for two G side units.

Step 6. Sew a G side unit to the remaining sides of the block center, again referring to Figure 7, to complete one Framed Square block; press seams toward the G side units. Repeat to make four blocks.

COMPLETING THE QUILT

Step 1. Sew a Framed Square block between two Ohio Star blocks to make a row; press seams toward Framed Square block. Repeat for two rows.

Step 2. Sew an Ohio Star block between two Framed Square blocks to make a row; press seams toward Framed Square blocks.

Step 3. Join the rows referring to the Placement Diagram for positioning; press seams in one direction.

Step 4. Referring to Figure 8, sew I to L along the

marked line; trim seam to ¼". Press I to the right side with seam toward I. Repeat with a second I square on the opposite end of L to complete an I-L unit; repeat to make four I-L units.

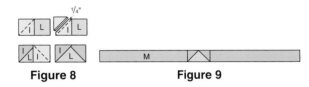

Figure 8   **Figure 9**

Step 5. Join two M strips with an I-L unit as shown in Figure 9; press seams toward M strips. Repeat to make four I-L-M strips.

Step 6. Sew an I-L-M strip to opposite sides of the pieced center; press seams toward I-L-M strips.

Step 7. Sew an N square to each end of the remaining I-L-M strips; press seams away from N. Repeat to make two strips.

Step 8. Sew the I-L-M-N strips to the remaining sides of the pieced center to complete the quilt top; press seams toward the I-L-M-N strips.

Step 9. Complete the quilt using the previously cut binding strips and referring to Completing Your Quilt on page 170. ●

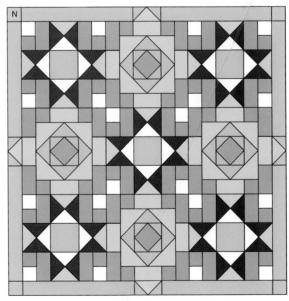

Southwest Stars
Placement Diagram
60" x 60"

design by **RHONDA TAYLOR**

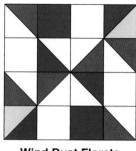

Wind Dust Florets
16" x 16" Block

Wind Dust Florets

Use three strong primary colors against a plain light background to produce the secondary twist with one simple pieced design.

PROJECT SPECIFICATIONS
Skill Level: Beginner
Quilt Size: 72" x 104"
Block Size: 16" x 16"
Number of Blocks: 24

MATERIALS
- 1⅛ yards yellow tonal
- 1⅜ yards red plaid
- 3 yards blue dot
- 3¼ yards white tonal
- Backing 78" x 110"
- Batting 78" x 110"
- All-purpose thread to match fabrics
- Quilting thread
- Basic sewing tools and supplies

CUTTING
Step 1. Cut (11) 4½" by fabric width strips white tonal; subcut six of the strips into (96) 4½" A squares.

Step 2. Cut (12) 4⅞" by fabric width strips white tonal; subcut strips into (96) 4⅞" C squares. Mark a diagonal line from corner to corner on the wrong side of each square.

Step 3. Cut (15) 4½" by fabric width strips blue dot; subcut six of the strips into (48) 4½" B squares. Set aside the remaining nine strips for G and H borders.

Step 4. Cut six 4⅞" by fabric width strips blue dot; subcut strips into (48) 4⅞" D squares.

Step 5. Cut three 4⅞" by fabric width strips yellow tonal; subcut strips into (24) 4⅞" E squares. Mark a diagonal line from corner to corner on the wrong side of each E square.

Step 6. Cut nine 2¼" by fabric width strips yellow tonal for binding.

Step 7. Cut nine 4⅞" by fabric width strips red plaid; subcut strips into (72) 4⅞" F squares.

PIECING THE BLOCKS

Step 1. Referring to Figure 1, place a C square right sides together with an F square; stitch ¼" on each side of the line. Cut apart on the marked line; press open with seam toward F to complete a C-F unit. Repeat with all F squares to make 144 C-F units.

Figure 1

Step 2. Repeat Step 1 with D and E squares to make 48 D-E units and with C and D squares to make 48 C-D units referring to Figure 2.

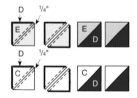

Figure 2

Step 3. To complete one block, join one each A and B square with one each C-F and D-E unit to make an X row as shown in Figure 3; press seams in one direction. Repeat to make two X rows.

Figure 3

Step 4. Join one A square with one C-D unit and two C-F units to make a Y row as shown in Figure 4; press seams in the opposite direction of the X row. Repeat to make two Y rows.

Figure 4

Step 5. Join one X and one Y row to make half a block as shown in Figure 5; press seam in one direction. Repeat for two block halves.

Figure 5

Wind Dust Florets
Placement Diagram
72" x 104"

Step 6. Join the two block halves to complete one Wind Dust Florets block referring to the block drawing; press seams in one direction. Repeat to make 24 blocks.

COMPLETING THE QUILT

Step 1. Join four blocks to make a row referring to Figure 6; press seams in one direction. Repeat to make six rows.

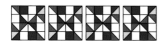

Figure 6

Step 2. Join the rows to complete the pieced center; press seams in one direction.

Step 3. Join the G and H strips on short ends to make one long strip; press seams open. Subcut strip into two 96½" G strips and two 72½" H strips.

Step 4. Sew a G strip to opposite long sides and H strips to the top and bottom of the pieced center; press seams toward G and H strips to complete the top.

Step 5. Complete the quilt using the previously cut binding strips and referring to Completing Your Quilt on page 170. ●

design by **SANDRA L. HATCH**

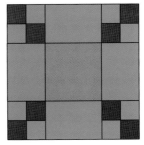

Four-Patch Variation
14" x 14" Block
Make 15

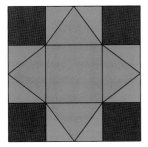

Amish Star
14" x 14" Block
Make 15

Amish Skies

Black fabric with dots, a twist on the black solid of Amish quilts, creates movement in this star-design bed quilt.

PROJECT SPECIFICATIONS

Skill Level: Beginner
Quilt Size: 88" x 102"
Block Size: 14" x 14"
Number of Blocks: 30

MATERIALS

All fabrics are batiks.

- ¾ yard black-with-pink dots
- 2½ yards pink embossed floral
- 3⅝ yards green metallic mottled
- 3⅝ yards black-with-green dots
- Backing 94" x 108"
- Batting 94" x 108"
- All-purpose thread to match fabrics
- Quilting thread
- Basic sewing tools and supplies

CUTTING

Step 1. Cut six 6½" by fabric width strips pink embossed floral; subcut three strips into (15) 6½" A squares. Set aside three strips for B-A-B strip sets.

Step 2. Cut seven 6½" by fabric width strips pink embossed floral; subcut strips into (60) 4½" E pieces.

Step 3. Cut six 4½" by fabric width B strips green metallic mottled.

Step 4. Cut four 6½" by fabric width strips green metallic mottled; subcut strips into (30) 4½" B rectangles.

Step 5. Cut seven 4½" by fabric width strips green metallic mottled; subcut strips into (120) 3⅜" F pieces. Draw a diagonal line from the bottom left to the upper right corner of 60 F pieces and from the bottom right to the upper left corner of the remaining F pieces for FR as shown in Figure 1.

Mark 60   Mark 60

Figure 1

Step 6. Cut eight 2½" by fabric width strips each green metallic mottled (C) and black-with-green dots (D).

Step 7. Cut eight 2½" by fabric width strips green metallic mottled. Join strips on short ends to make one long strip; press seams open. Subcut strip into two 86½" J strips and two 76½" K strips.

Step 8. Cut seven 4½" by fabric width strips black-with-green dots; subcut strips into (60) 4½" G squares.

Step 9. Cut eight 1½" by fabric width strips black-with-green dots. Join strips on short ends to make one long strip; press seams open. Subcut strip into two 84½" H strips and two 72½" I strips.

Step 10. Cut nine 6½" by fabric width strips black-with-green dots. Join strips on short ends to make one long strip; press seams open. Subcut strip into two 90½" L strips and two 88½" M strips.

Step 11. Cut (10) 2¼" by fabric width strips black-with-pink dots for binding.

PIECING THE AMISH STAR BLOCKS

Step 1. Place an F rectangle right sides together with E, matching one corner of F with the corner of E and placing the opposite corner of F where it touches the top edge of E as shown in Figure 2; stitch on the marked line. Before trimming, finger-press F to the right side to be sure it covers the corner of E.

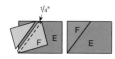

Figure 2	**Figure 3**

Step 2. Trim the F part of the stitched unit ¼" beyond the stitched line and press F to the right side as shown in Figure 3. **Note:** *Leaving the E base creates stability and takes care of any inaccuracies that might occur using this method.*

Step 3. Repeat Steps 1 and 2 with FR on the opposite end of E as shown in Figure 4 to complete an E-F unit. Repeat to make 60 E-F units.

Step 4. Sew an E-F unit to opposite sides of A to

complete the center row as shown in Figure 5; press seams toward A.

Figure 4	**Figure 5**

Step 5. Sew a G square to opposite sides of an E-F unit to complete the top row as shown in Figure 6; press seams toward G. Repeat to make the bottom row.

Figure 6

Step 6. Sew the center row between the top and bottom rows to complete one Amish Star block referring to the block drawing for positioning of rows; press seams away from the center row. Repeat to make 15 blocks.

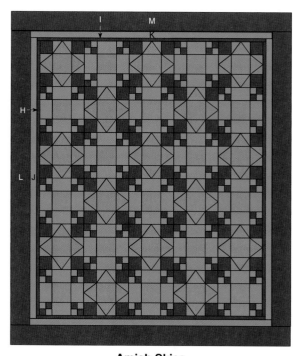

Amish Skies
Placement Diagram
88" x 102"

COMPLETING THE FOUR-PATCH VARIATION BLOCKS

Step 1. Sew a C strip to a D strip with right sides together along the length; press seam toward D strip. Repeat to make eight C-D strip sets.

Step 2. Subcut C-D strip sets into (120) 2½" C-D units as shown in Figure 7.

Figure 7   **Figure 8**

Step 3. Sew a B strip to opposite sides of an A strip with right sides together along the length; press seams toward B strips. Repeat to make three B-A-B strip sets.

Step 4. Subcut the B-A-B strip sets into (15) 6½" B-A-B units as shown in Figure 8.

Step 5. Join two C-D units to make a corner unit as shown in Figure 9; press seam to one side. Repeat to make 60 corner units.

Figure 9   **Figure 10**

Step 6. To complete one Four-Patch Variation block, sew a corner unit to opposite ends of B to make the top row as shown in Figure 10; press seams toward B. Repeat to make the bottom row.

Step 7. Sew a B-A-B unit between the top and bottom rows to complete one block referring to the block drawing; press seams toward the B-A-B unit. Repeat to make 15 blocks.

COMPLETING THE QUILT

Step 1. Join three Amish Star blocks with two Four-Patch Variation blocks to make a row as shown in Figure 11; press seams toward Four-Patch Variation blocks. Repeat to make three rows.

Step 2. Join three Four-Patch Variation blocks with two Amish Star blocks to make a row, again referring to Figure 11; press seams toward Four-Patch Variation blocks. Repeat to make three rows.

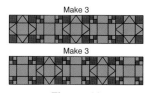

Figure 11

Step 3. Join the rows referring to the Placement Diagram for positioning of rows; press seams in one direction.

Step 4. Sew an H strip to opposite long sides and I strips to the top and bottom of the pieced center; press seams toward H and I strips.

Step 5. Sew J strips to opposite long sides and K strips to the top and bottom of the pieced center; press seams toward J and K strips.

Step 6. Sew L strips to opposite long sides and M strips to the top and bottom of the pieced center to complete the quilt top; press seams toward L and M strips.

Step 7. Complete the quilt using the previously cut binding strips and referring to Completing Your Quilt on page 170. ●

design by **JULIE WEAVER**

Holiday Splendor
12" x 12" Block

Holiday Splendor

Combining a block called Odds 'n' Ends with a simple sash

creates an interesting and surprising finish—a quilt that looks

intricate but is easy enough to be considered a beginner project.

PROJECT SPECIFICATIONS

Skill Level: Beginner
Quilt Size: 84½" x 98"
Block Size: 12" x 12"
Number of Blocks: 20

MATERIALS

- 1¼ yards green print
- 1⅓ yards green tonal
- 1½ yards cream print
- 1¾ yards red tonal
- 3⅔ yards green floral
- Backing 91" x 104"
- Batting 91" x 104"
- Neutral color all-purpose thread
- Quilting thread
- Basic sewing tools and supplies

CUTTING

Step 1. Cut two 3⅞" by fabric width strips cream print; subcut strips into (20) 3⅞" A squares. Draw a diagonal line from corner to corner on the wrong side of each A square.

Step 2. Cut four 3½" by fabric width strips cream print; subcut strips into (40) 3½" B squares.

Step 3. Cut (14) 2" by fabric width G strips cream print.

Step 4. Cut two 3⅞" by fabric width strips red tonal; subcut strips into (20) 3⅞" C squares.

Step 5. Cut (25) 2" by fabric width strips red tonal; subcut two strips into (30) 2" I squares. Set aside eight strips for D-E strip sets. Join the remaining strips on short ends to make one long strip; press seams in one direction. Subcut strip into two 69½" J strips, two 59" K strips, two 89½" N strips and two 79" O strips.

Step 6. Cut (22) 2" by fabric width strips green tonal for E and F.

Step 7. Cut (17) 2" by fabric width strips green print; subcut strips into (49) 12½" H strips.

Step 8. Cut eight 9" by fabric width strips green floral. Join strips on short ends to make one long strip; press seams open. Subcut strip into two 72½" L strips and two 76" M strips.

Step 9. Cut nine 3½" by fabric width strips green floral. Join strips on short ends to make one long strip; press seams open. Subcut strip into two 92½" P strips and two 85" Q strips.

Step 10. Cut (10) 2¼" by fabric width strips green floral for binding.

PIECING THE BLOCKS

Step 1. Referring to Figure 1, place an A square right sides together with C; stitch ¼" on each side of the marked line. Cut apart on the marked line; press open with seams toward C to complete two A-C units. Repeat with all A and C squares to complete 40 A-C units.

Figure 1

Step 2. Sew a D strip to an E strip with right sides together along the length; press seam toward D. Repeat to make eight strip sets.

Step 3. Subcut the D-E strip sets into (160) 2" D-E units as shown in Figure 2.

Figure 2

Step 4. Sew an F strip to a G strip with right sides together along the length; press seams toward F. Repeat for 14 F-G strip sets.

Step 5. Subcut the F-G strip sets into (80) 6½" F-G units as shown in Figure 3.

Figure 3

Step 6. To complete one Holiday Splendor block, sew B to the C side of an A-C unit as shown in Figure 4; press seam toward B. Repeat to make two A-C-B units.

Figure 4   **Figure 5**

Step 7. Join the two A-C-B units to complete the center unit as shown in Figure 5; press seam in one direction.

Step 8. Sew an F-G unit to opposite sides of the center unit to make the center row as shown in Figure 6; press seams toward the F-G units.

Figure 6

Step 9. Join two D-E units to make a Four-Patch unit as shown in Figure 7; press seam to one side. Repeat to make four units.

Figure 7

Step 10. Sew a Four-Patch unit to opposite ends of an F-G unit as shown in Figure 8; press seams toward the F-G unit. Repeat to make two end rows.

Figure 8

Step 11. Sew an end row to the remaining sides of the center row to complete one block referring to the block drawing for positioning; press seams away from the center row. Repeat to make 20 blocks.

COMPLETING THE QUILT

Step 1. Join four Holiday Splendor blocks with five H strips to make a block row as shown in Figure 9; press seams toward H. Repeat to make five block rows.

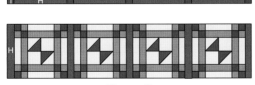

Figure 9

Step 2. Join five I squares with four H strips to make a sashing row, again referring to Figure 9; press seams toward H. Repeat to make six sashing rows.

Step 3. Join the sashing rows with the block rows referring to the Placement Diagram for positioning of rows; press seams toward the sashing rows.

Step 4. Sew a J strip to opposite long sides and K strips to the top and bottom of the pieced center; press seams toward J and K strips.

Step 5. Sew an L strip to opposite long sides and M strips to the top and bottom of the pieced center; press seams toward L and M strips.

Step 6. Sew an N strip to opposite long sides and O strips to the top and bottom of the pieced center; press seams toward N and O strips.

Step 7. Sew a P strip to opposite long sides and Q strips to the top and bottom of the pieced center to complete the quilt top; press seams toward P and Q strips.

Step 8. Complete the quilt using the previously cut binding strips and referring to Completing Your Quilt on page 170. ●

Holiday Splendor
Placement Diagram
84½" x 98"

design by **SUE HARVEY & SANDY BOOBAR**

Midnight Star
9" x 9" Block
Make 17

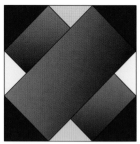

The House That Jack Built
9" x 9" Block
Make 18

Midnight Paths

The edges of the Midnight Star and The House That Jack Built blocks are blurred as the pieces combine to form dark pathways across this quilt.

PROJECT SPECIFICATIONS
Skill Level: Intermediate
Quilt Size: 66" x 84"
Block Size: 9" x 9"
Number of Blocks: 35

MATERIALS
All fabrics are batiks.
- ⅝ yard cream print
- 1¼ yards taupe mottled
- 1⅓ yards dark green mottled
- 1⅔ yards purple dot
- 3⅜ yards rose print
- Backing 72" x 90"
- Batting 72" x 90"
- Neutral color all-purpose thread
- Quilting thread
- Basic sewing tools and supplies

CUTTING
Step 1. Cut three 9" by fabric width strips rose print; subcut strips into (18) 4¾" A rectangles.

Step 2. Cut three 4¾" by fabric width strips rose print; subcut strips into (36) 2⅝" B rectangles.

Step 3. Cut two strips each 6½" x 72½" (O) and 6½" x 66½" (P) along remaining length of rose print.

Step 4. Cut four 3⅞" by fabric width strips purple dot; subcut strips into (36) 3⅞" squares. Cut each square in half on one diagonal to make 72 C triangles.

Step 5. Cut four 4¼" by fabric width strips purple dot; subcut strips into (34) 4¼" squares. Cut each square on both diagonals to make 136 H triangles.

Step 6. Cut six 3½" by fabric width K/L strips purple dot.

Step 7. Cut two 4¼" by fabric width strips taupe mottled; subcut strips into (18) 4¼" squares. Cut each square on both diagonals to make 70 D triangles; discard two remaining triangles.

Step 8. Cut four 3⅞" by fabric width strips taupe

mottled; subcut strips into (34) 3⅞" I squares.

Step 9. Cut six 2" by fabric width M/N strips taupe mottled.

Step 10. Cut two 4¼" by fabric width strips cream print; subcut strips into (18) 4¼" squares. Cut each square on both diagonals to make 70 E triangles; discard two remaining triangles.

Step 11. Cut three 2⅝" by fabric width strips each cream print (G) and dark green mottled (F).

Step 12. Cut four 3⅞" by fabric width strips dark green mottled; subcut strips into (34) 3⅞" J squares.

Step 13. Cut eight 2¼" by fabric width strips dark green mottled for binding.

PIECING THE HOUSE THAT JACK BUILT BLOCKS

Step 1. Sew C to each short end of each A rectangle as shown in Figure 1; press seams toward C.

Figure 1

Step 2. Sew D to one end and E to the opposite end of each B rectangle, again referring to Figure 1; press seams away from B.

Step 3. Sew C to each B unit, again referring to Figure 1; press seams toward C.

Step 4. Sew an A unit between two B units to complete one The House That Jack Built block referring to the block drawing for positioning; press seams away from the A unit. Repeat to make 18 blocks.

PIECING THE MIDNIGHT STAR BLOCKS

Step 1. Sew a G strip to an F strip with right sides together along length; press seam toward F. Repeat for three strip sets.

Step 2. Subcut the strip sets into (34) 2⅝" F-G units as shown in Figure 2.

Figure 2   **Figure 3**

Step 3. Join two F-G units to complete a center unit as shown in Figure 3; press seam in one direction. Repeat to make 17 center units.

Step 4. Draw a diagonal line from corner to corner on the wrong side of each I square.

Step 5. Place I right sides together with J; stitch ¼" on each side of the marked line, cut on the marked line and press I open to complete two I-J units as shown in Figure 4; repeat to make 68 I-J units.

Figure 4   **Figure 5**

Step 6. Sew H to D and H to E as shown in Figure 5; press seams toward D and E. Repeat to make 34 each D-H and E-H units.

Step 7. Sew a D-H and E-H unit to the I sides of 34 I-J units to make corner units as shown in Figure 6; press seams away from I-J.

Figure 6

Step 8. Sew H to the I sides of the remaining I-J units as shown in Figure 7; press seams toward H.

Figure 7

Figure 8

Step 9. Sew an H-I-J unit to opposite sides of the center units to make 17 center rows as shown in Figure 8; press seams toward the center units.

Step 10. Sew a corner unit to opposite sides of the center rows to complete the Midnight Star blocks referring to the block drawing for positioning; press seams toward the corner units.

COMPLETING THE QUILT

Step 1. Join three The House That Jack Built blocks with two Midnight Star blocks to make a row as shown in Figure 9; press seams toward The House That Jack Built blocks. Repeat to make four rows.

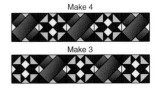

Make 4

Make 3

Figure 9

Step 2. Join three Midnight Star blocks with two The House That Jack Built blocks to make a row, again referring to Figure 9; press seams toward The House That Jack Built blocks. Repeat to make three rows.

Step 3. Join the rows to complete the pieced center referring to the Placement Diagram for positioning; press seams in one direction.

Step 4. Join the K/L strips on short ends to make a long strip; press seams to one side. Subcut the strip into two 63½" K strips and two 51½" L strips.

Step 5. Sew the K strips to opposite long sides and the L strips to the top and bottom of the pieced center; press seams toward the K and L strips.

Step 6. Join the M/N strips on short ends to make a long strip; press seams to one side. Subcut the strip into two 69½" M strips and two 54½" N strips.

Step 7. Sew the M strips to opposite long sides and the N strips to the top and bottom of the pieced center; press seams toward M and N strips.

Step 8. Sew the O strips to opposite long sides and the P strips to the top and bottom of the pieced center to complete the top; press seams toward O and P strips.

Step 9. Complete the quilt using the previously cut binding strips and referring to Completing Your Quilt on page 170. ●

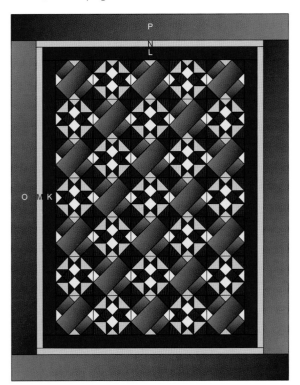

Midnight Paths
Placement Diagram
66" x 84"

design by **JUDITH SANDSTROM**

Cummerbund A
15" x 15" Block
Make 4

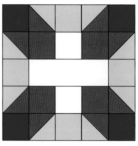

Cummerbund B
15" x 15" Block
Make 1

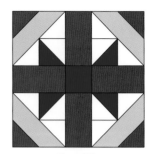

Bow Tie
15" x 15" Block
Make 4

Black Tie

Three unrelated classic blocks combine to make a formal black tie and cummerbund mosaic.

PROJECT SPECIFICATIONS

Skill Level: Beginner
Quilt Size: 45" x 45"
Block Size: 15" x 15"
Number of Blocks: 9

MATERIALS

- ⅔ yard red tonal
- ¾ yard white tonal
- 1 yard tan tonal
- 1⅛ yards black tonal
- Backing 51" x 51"
- Batting 51" x 51"
- All-purpose thread to match fabrics
- Quilting thread
- Basic sewing tools and supplies

CUTTING

Step 1. Cut three 3½" by fabric width strips white tonal; subcut one strip into (12) 3½" B squares. Subcut one strip into four 9½" A pieces; set aside the remaining strip for B-C units.

Step 2. Cut three 3⅞" by fabric width strips white tonal; subcut strips into (24) 3⅞" I squares.

From the remainder of one strip, cut one 3½" x 9½" A piece. Cut each I square in half on one diagonal to make 48 I triangles.

Step 3. Cut seven 3½" by fabric width strips black tonal; set aside two C strips for B-C units. Subcut three strips into (16) 6½" L pieces. Subcut the remaining strips into (16) 3½" J squares. Draw a diagonal line from corner to corner on the wrong side of each square.

Step 4. Cut two 3⅞" by fabric width strips black tonal; subcut strips into (20) 3⅞" squares. Cut each square in half on one diagonal to make 40 E triangles.

Step 5. Cut two 3½" by fabric width strips tan tonal; subcut strips into (20) 3½" F squares.

Step 6. Cut two 3⅞" by fabric width strips tan tonal; subcut strips into (20) 3⅞" squares. Cut each square in half on one diagonal to make 40 D triangles.

Step 7. Cut two 6⅞" by fabric width strips tan tonal; subcut strips into eight 6⅞" squares. Cut each square in half on one diagonal to make 16 K triangles.

Step 8. Cut one 3½" by fabric width strip red

tonal; subcut strip into (12) 3½" G squares.

Step 9. Cut one 3⅞" by fabric width strip red tonal; subcut strip into eight 3⅞" squares. Cut each square in half on one diagonal to make 16 H triangles.

Step 10. Cut five 2¼" by fabric width strips red tonal for binding.

PIECING THE CUMMERBUND A BLOCKS

Step 1. Sew the B strip between two C strips with right sides together along the length; press seams toward C strips. Subcut strip set into (10) 3½" B-C units as shown in Figure 1. Set aside two units for Cummerbund B blocks.

| **Figure 1** | **Figure 2** |

Step 2. Sew D to E to make a D-E unit as shown in Figure 2; press seam toward E. Repeat to make 40 D-E units. Set aside eight D-E units for Cummerbund B blocks.

Step 3. To complete one Cummerbund A block, join two B squares with one F square and two D-E units to make an F row as shown in Figure 3; press seams toward B and F.

| **Figure 3** | **Figure 4** |

Step 4. Join two D-E units with a B-C unit to make a B row as shown in Figure 4; press seams toward the B-C unit. Repeat to make two B rows.

Step 5. Sew F to each short end of A to make an A row; press seams toward F.

Step 6. Join two D-E units with one each B, F and G squares to make a G row as shown in Figure 5; press seams away from the D-E units.

Figure 5

Step 7. Arrange the rows and join as shown in Figure 6 to complete one Cummerbund A block; press seams in one direction. Repeat to make four blocks.

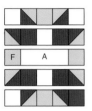

Figure 6

COMPLETING THE CUMMERBUND B BLOCKS

Step 1. Piece rows as for the Cummerbund A blocks, substituting G squares for B squares in the corners of the F and G rows referring to Figure 7.

| **Figure 7** | **Figure 8** |

Step 2. Arrange the rows and join as shown in Figure 8 to complete one Cummerbund B block; press seams in one direction.

Black Tie
Placement Diagram
45" x 45"

COMPLETING THE BOW TIE BLOCKS

Step 1. Sew H to I as shown in Figure 9; press seam toward H. Sew I to two adjacent sides of the pieced unit to make an H-I unit, again referring to Figure 9; press seams toward I. Repeat to make 16 H-I units.

Figure 9

Step 2. Referring to Figure 10, place J right sides together with K; stitch on the marked line. Trim seam to ¼" and press J to the right side to complete a J-K unit; repeat to make 16 J-K units.

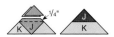

Figure 10   **Figure 11**

Step 3. To complete one Black Tie block, sew an H-I unit to a J-K unit to make a corner unit as shown in Figure 11; press seams toward the J-K unit. Repeat to make four corner units.

Step 4. Join two corner units with L to complete an L unit as shown in Figure 12; press seams toward L. Repeat to make two L units.

Figure 12

Step 5. Join two L pieces with G to make a G unit referring to Figure 13; press seams toward L pieces.

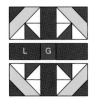

Figure 13

Step 6. Sew the G unit between two L units, again referring to Figure 13 to complete one Bow Tie block; press seams toward the G unit. Repeat to make four blocks.

COMPLETING THE QUILT

Step 1. Join two Cummerbund A blocks with one Bow Tie block to make the top row referring to the Placement Diagram for positioning of blocks; repeat for the bottom row. Press seams toward the Cummerband A blocks.

Step 2. Join two Bow Tie blocks with the Cummerbund B block to complete the center row; press seams toward the Cummerbund B block.

Step 3. Join the rows to complete the pieced top; press seams in one direction.

Step 4. Complete the quilt using the previously cut binding strips and referring to Completing Your Quilt on page 170. ●

design by **CATE TALLMAN-EVANS**

Puss in the Corner
9" x 9" Block
Make 18

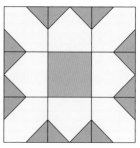

Prairie Flower
9" x 9" Block
Make 17

Prairie Garden

Puss in the Corner and Prairie Flower blocks are combined to create a formal garden of beautiful roses and foliage. Parts of the Prairie Flower blocks are colored to add petals and dimension to the pieced roses primarily made from the Puss in the Corner blocks. A lush, green backdrop for the pieced roses is found in the colors of the Prairie Flower block.

PROJECT SPECIFICATIONS
Skill Level: Intermediate
Quilt Size: 60" x 78"
Block Size: 9" x 9"
Number of Blocks: 35

MATERIALS
- ⅓ yard dark green tonal
- ½ yard olive green tonal
- ⅞ yard tan tonal
- ⅞ yard light mauve tonal
- 1¼ yards dark mauve tonal
- 1⅓ yards light green print
- 1½ yards cream floral
- 1⅝ yards medium mauve tonal

- Backing 66" x 84"
- Batting 66" x 84"
- Neutral color all-purpose thread
- Quilting thread
- Basic sewing tools and supplies

CUTTING
Step 1. Cut two 3½" by fabric width strips tan tonal; subcut strips into (18) 3½" A squares.
Step 2. Cut seven 2¼" by fabric width strips tan tonal for binding.
Step 3. Cut (12) 2" by fabric width strips light mauve tonal; subcut strips into (144) 3½" B pieces.
Step 4. Cut (20) 2" by fabric width strips

medium mauve tonal; subcut strips into (416) 2" C squares. Mark a diagonal line from corner to corner on the wrong side of each square.

Step 5. Cut five 2⅜" by fabric width strips medium mauve tonal; subcut strips into (72) 2⅜" squares. Cut each square in half on one diagonal to make 144 F triangles.

Step 6. Cut four 3⅞" by fabric width strips dark mauve tonal; subcut strips into (36) 3⅞" squares. Cut each square in half on one diagonal to make 72 D triangles.

Step 7. Cut (11) 2" by fabric width strips dark mauve tonal; subcut strips into (216) 2" E squares. Mark a diagonal line from corner to corner on 144 of the E squares.

Step 8. Cut two 3½" by fabric width strips dark green tonal; subcut strips into (17) 3½" G squares.

Step 9. Cut (12) 3½" by fabric width strips light green print; subcut strips into (136) 3½" H squares.

Step 10. Cut six 2" by fabric width strips olive green tonal. Join strips on short ends to make one long strip; press seams open. Subcut strip into two 63½" I strips and two 48½" J strips.

Step 11. Cut seven 6½" by fabric width strips cream floral. Join strips on short ends to make one long strip; press seams open. Subcut strip into two 66½" K strips and two 60½" L strips.

PIECING THE PUSS IN THE CORNER BLOCKS

Step 1. Referring to Figure 1, place C right sides together with B; stitch on the marked line. Trim seam to ¼"; press C to the right side. Repeat on the opposite end of B to complete a B-C unit. Repeat to make 72 B-C units.

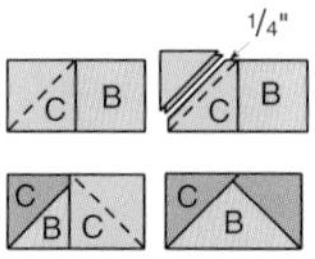

Figure 1

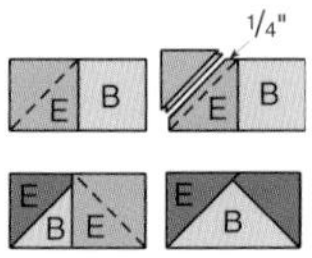

Figure 2

Step 2. Repeat Step 1 with B pieces and E squares to complete 72 B-E units referring to Figure 2.

Step 3. Sew F to two adjacent sides of E as shown in Figure 3; press seams toward F. Repeat to make 72 E-F units.

Figure 3

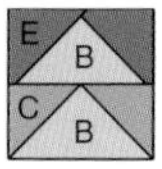

Figure 4

Step 4. Sew D to each E-F unit to make 72 corner units; press seams toward D.

Step 5. To complete one block, sew a B-C unit to a B-E unit to make a side unit as shown in Figure 4; press seam toward B-E unit. Repeat to make four side units.

Step 6. Sew a side unit to opposite sides of A to make the center row as shown in Figure 5; press seams toward A.

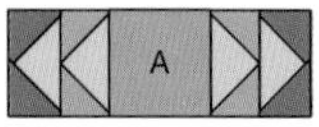

Figure 5

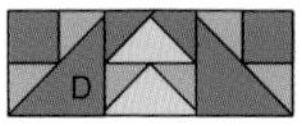

Figure 6

Step 7. Sew a corner unit to opposite sides of a side unit to make a top row as shown in Figure 6; press seams toward corner units. Repeat to make the bottom row.

Step 8. Sew the center row between the top and bottom rows to complete one Puss in the Corner block referring to the block drawing; press seams in one direction. Repeat to make 18 blocks.

COMPLETING THE PRAIRIE FLOWER BLOCKS

Step 1. Referring to Figure 7, sew C to opposite corners of H; trim seams to ¼". Press C to the right side to complete a corner C-H unit; repeat to make 68 corner C-H units.

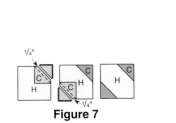
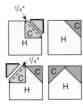

Figure 7   **Figure 8**

Step 2. Referring to Figure 8, sew C to two adjacent sides of H; trim seams to ¼". Press C to the right side to complete a side C-H unit; repeat to make 68 side C-H units.

Step 3. To complete one block, sew a side C-H unit to opposite sides of G to complete the center row as shown in Figure 9; press seams toward G.

Figure 9

Step 4. Sew a corner C-H unit to opposite sides of a side C-H unit to make the top row, again referring to Figure 9; press seams toward the corner C-H units. Repeat to make the bottom row.

Step 5. Sew the center row between the top and bottom rows referring to the block drawing to complete one Prairie Flower block; press seams in one direction. Repeat to make 17 blocks.

COMPLETING THE QUILT

Step 1. Join three Puss in the Corner blocks with two Prairie Flower blocks to make an X row as shown in Figure 10; press seams toward the Prairie Flower blocks. Repeat to make four X rows.

Step 2. Join three Prairie Flower blocks with two Puss in the Corner blocks to make a Y row, again referring to Figure 10; press seams toward

the Prairie Flower blocks. Repeat to make three Y rows.

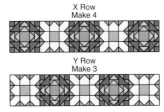

Figure 10

Step 3. Join the rows referring to the Placement Diagram for positioning; press seams in one direction.

Step 4. Sew I strips to opposite long sides and J strips to the top and bottom of the pieced center; press seams toward I and J strips.

Step 5. Sew K strips to opposite long sides and L strips to the top and bottom of the pieced center; press seams toward K and L strips.

Step 6. Complete the quilt using the previously cut binding strips and referring to Completing Your Quilt on page 170. ●

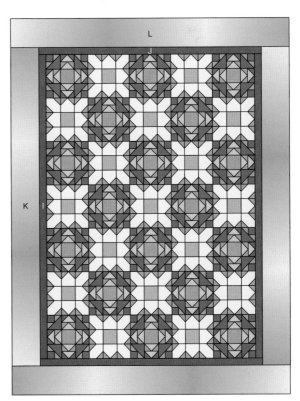

Prairie Garden
Placement Diagram
60" x 78"

design by **LUCY A. FAZELY & MICHAEL L. BURNS**

Night & Day
8" x 8" Block
Make 18

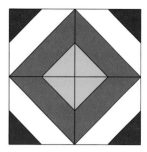

Mosaic
8" x 8" Block
Make 17

Garden Affair

The Night & Day and Mosaic blocks come together to make a lattice of purple strips with a strong diagonal influence.

PROJECT SPECIFICATIONS

Skill Level: Intermediate
Quilt Size: 56" x 72"
Block Size: 8" x 8"
Number of Blocks: 35

MATERIALS

- ½ yard gold print
- ¾ yard yellow bee print
- ¾ yard blue swirl
- 1½ yards cream print
- 1⅝ yards purple print
- 2⅜ yards red bee print
- Backing 62" x 78"
- Batting 62" x 78"
- All-purpose thread to match fabrics
- Quilting thread
- Template plastic
- Basic sewing tools and supplies

CUTTING

Step 1. Cut seven 2" by fabric width strips gold print; subcut strips into (68) 4" A pieces.

Step 2. Cut (12) 2" by fabric width strips red bee print; subcut strips into (68) 6½" B pieces.

Step 3. Cut six 6½" by fabric width strips red bee print. Join strips on short ends to make one long strip; press seams open. Subcut strip into two 60½" K strips and two 56½" L strips.

Step 4. Cut seven 2¼" by fabric width strips red bee print for binding.

Step 5. Cut (12) 2" by fabric width strips cream print; subcut strips into (68) 6½" C pieces.

Step 6. Cut (16) 1½" by fabric width strips cream print; subcut strips into (144) 4½" H pieces.

Step 7. Cut seven 2" by fabric width strips purple print; subcut strips into (68) 4" D pieces.

Step 8. Cut (16) 1½" by fabric width strips purple print; subcut strips into (144) 4½" F pieces.

Step 9. Cut five 2½" by fabric width strips purple print. Join strips on short ends to make one long strip; press seams open. Subcut strip into two 56½" I strips and two 44½" J strips.

Step 10. Cut (12) 1¾" by fabric width strips yellow bee print; subcut strips into (144) 3½" E pieces.

Step 6. Join two block quarters to complete half the block; press seam in one direction. Repeat and press seam in opposite direction. Join the two halves referring to the block drawing to complete one Mosaic block; press seam in one direction. Repeat to make 17 blocks.

PIECING THE NIGHT & DAY BLOCKS

Step 1. Prepare a template for the Y piece using pattern given.

Step 2. Center and sew E to F as shown in Figure 5; press seam toward E. Repeat with all E and F pieces to complete 144 E-F units.

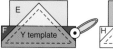

Figure 5   **Figure 6**

Step 11. Cut (12) 1¾" by fabric width strips blue swirl; subcut strips into (144) 3½" G pieces.

Step 3. Using the Y template, trim E-F units as shown in Figure 6.

Step 4. Repeat Steps 1–3 with G and H pieces and trim with the Y template, again referring to Figure 6.

PIECING THE MOSAIC BLOCKS

Step 1. Prepare a template for the X piece using pattern given.

Step 2. Center and sew A to B as shown in Figure 1; press seam toward B. Repeat with all A and B pieces to complete 68 A-B units.

Step 5. To complete one Night & Day block, join one E-F and one G-H unit as shown in Figure 7; repeat to complete four units and four reversed units. Press seams in the units toward the E-F units and in the reversed units toward the G-H units.

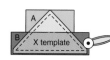

Figure 1   **Figure 2**

Figure 7   **Figure 8**

Step 3. Using the X template, trim A-B units as shown in Figure 2.

Step 4. Repeat Steps 1–3 with C and D pieces and trim with the X template as shown in Figure 3.

Step 6. Join one unit and one reversed unit to complete a block quarter as shown in Figure 8; repeat for four block quarters. Press seams in two units in one direction and in the remaining two units in the opposite direction.

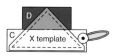

Figure 3   **Figure 4**

Step 5. To complete one Mosaic block, join one A-B unit with one C-D unit to make a block quarter as shown in Figure 4; press seam toward B. Repeat to make four block quarters.

Step 7. Join two block quarters to complete half the block; press seam in one direction. Repeat and press seam in opposite direction. Join the two halves referring to the block drawing to complete one Night & Day block; press seam in one direction. Repeat to make 18 blocks.

COMPLETING THE QUILT

Step 1. Join three Night & Day blocks with two Mosaic blocks to make an X row as shown in Figure 9; press seams toward Mosaic blocks. Repeat to make four X rows.

Step 2. Join three Mosaic blocks with two Night & Day blocks to make a Y row, again referring to Figure 9; press seams toward Mosaic blocks. Repeat to make three Y rows.

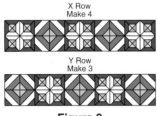

X Row
Make 4

Y Row
Make 3

Figure 9

Garden Affair
Placement Diagram
56" x 72"

Step 3. Arrange and join the X and Y rows referring to the Placement Diagram for positioning; press seams in one direction.

Step 4. Sew I strips to opposite long sides and J strips to the top and bottom of the pieced center; press seams toward I and J strips.

Step 5. Sew K strips to opposite long sides and L strips to the top and bottom of the pieced center to complete the quilt; press seams toward K and L strips.

Step 6. Complete the quilt using the previously cut binding strips and referring to Completing Your Quilt on page 170. ●

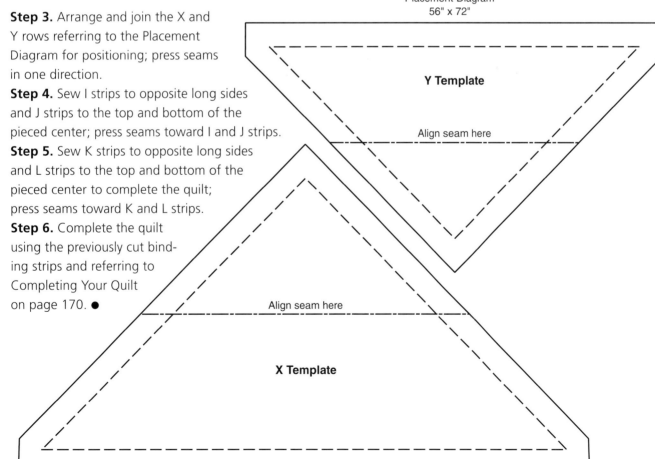

Y Template

Align seam here

Align seam here

X Template

design by **JULIE WEAVER**

Maple Leaf Cluster
12" x 12" Block

Autumn Air

Four traditional Maple Leaf blocks are joined to make a Maple Leaf Cluster block. Joining these blocks without sashing creates an unexpected intricate path through the fallen leaves.

PROJECT SPECIFICATIONS
Skill Level: Beginner
Quilt Size: 74" x 86"
Block Size: 12" x 12"
Number of Blocks: 20

MATERIALS
- ½ yard each 10 different batik prints
- 1½ yards brown print
- 2 yards brown mottled
- 2 yards cream mottled
- Backing 80" x 92"
- Batting 80" x 92"
- All-purpose thread to match fabrics
- Quilting thread
- Basic sewing tools and supplies

CUTTING
Step 1. Cut five 2½" by fabric width strips brown print; subcut strips into (80) 2½" A squares.
Step 2. Cut (12) 2⅞" by fabric width strips brown print; subcut strips into (160) 2⅞" F squares.
Step 3. Cut eight 2" by fabric width strips cream mottled; subcut strips into (160) 2" B squares. Draw a diagonal line from corner to corner on the wrong side of each square.
Step 4. Cut (12) 2⅞" by fabric width strips cream mottled; subcut strips into (160) 2⅞" E squares. Draw a diagonal line from corner to corner on the wrong side of each square.
Step 5. Cut five 2½" by fabric width strips cream mottled; subcut strips into (80) 2½" G squares.
Step 6. From each batik, cut eight 2½" C squares and eight 2½" x 4½" D rectangles.
Step 7. Cut a total of 58 assorted 4½" x 9½" J rectangles from the 10 batiks.
Step 8. Cut six 2½" by fabric width strips brown mottled. Join strips on short ends to make one long strip; press seams open. Subcut strip into two 60½" H strips and two 52½" I strips.
Step 9. Cut four 9½" x 9½" K squares brown mottled.

Step 10. Cut eight 2½" by fabric width strips brown mottled. Join strips on short ends to make one long strip; press seams open. Subcut strip into two 82½" L strips and two 74½" M strips.

Step 11. Cut eight 2¼" by fabric width strips brown mottled for binding.

PIECING THE BLOCKS

Step 1. Referring to Figure 1, place a B square right sides together on one corner of A; stitch on the marked line. Trim seam to ¼"; press B to the right side. Repeat with a second B on the opposite corner of A to complete an A-B unit as shown in Figure 2. Repeat to make 80 A-B units.

Figure 1   **Figure 2**

Step 2. Place an E square right sides together with F; stitch ¼" on each side of the marked line as shown in Figure 3.

Figure 3

Step 3. Cut the stitched unit apart on the drawn line to create two E-F units, again referring to Figure 3. Repeat with all E and F squares to make 320 E-F units.

Step 4. To complete one Maple Leaf Cluster block, select four matching C squares and D rectangles. Sew C to an A-B unit and add D as shown in Figure 4; press seams toward C and D. Repeat to make four A-B-C-D units.

Figure 4

Step 5. Join two E-F units as shown in Figure 5; press seams in one direction. Repeat to make four E-F units and four reversed E-F units. Add G to the F end of the reversed units, again referring to Figure 5; press seams toward G.

Make 4

Reversed
Make 4

G

Figure 5

Step 6. Sew an E-F and an E-F-G unit to the A-B-C-D unit to complete one leaf unit as shown in Figure 6; press seams away from the E-F units. Repeat to make four leaf units.

Figure 6

Step 7. Join four leaf units to complete one Maple Leaf Cluster block referring to the block drawing; press seams in one direction. Repeat to make 20 blocks.

COMPLETING THE QUILT

Step 1. Arrange the blocks in five rows of four blocks each. Join the blocks in rows; press seams in one direction. Join the rows to complete the pieced center; press seams in one direction.

Step 2. Sew H strips to opposite long sides and I strips to the top and bottom of the pieced center; press seams toward H and I strips.

Step 3. Select and join 16 J rectangles on the 9½" sides to make a J side strip; press seams in one direction. Repeat to make two J side strips. Sew the J side strips to opposite long sides of the pieced center; press seams toward H strips.

Step 4. Select and join 13 J rectangles to make a J top strip; press seams in one direction. Repeat to make the J bottom strip.

Step 5. Sew a K square to each end of the J top and J bottom strips; press seams toward K. Sew

these strips to the top and bottom of the pieced center; press seams toward I strips.

Step 6. Sew L strips to opposite long sides and M strips to the top and bottom of the pieced center to complete the quilt top; press seams toward L and M strips.

Step 7. Complete the quilt using the previously cut binding strips and referring to Completing Your Quilt on page 170. ●

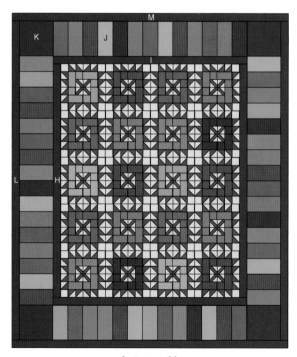

Autumn Air
Placement Diagram
74" x 86"

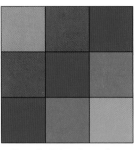

Purple/Blue Impulse
12" x 12" Block
Make 12

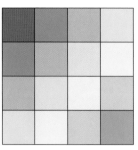

Blue/Green Impulse
12" x 12" Block
Make 12

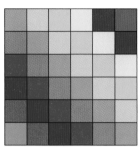

Orange/Red/Green Impulse
12" x 12" Block
Make 12

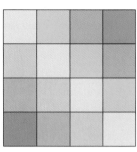

Red/Purple Impulse
12" x 12" Block
Make 12

Impulse

The traditional Trip Around the World design uses all the same-size squares to create the rounds. In this quilt, the trip is created with three different-size squares in colorful blocks.

PROJECT SPECIFICATIONS

Skill Level: Beginner
Quilt Size: 88" x 112"
Block Size: 12" x 12"
Number of Blocks: 48

MATERIALS

- ¼ yard each very dark green (A), dark green (B), medium green (C), dark red (G), medium red (H), light red (I), light blue (N) and medium purple (R)
- ⅓ yard each very dark red (F) and light gold (Z)
- ⅜ yard each light green (D), pale red (J), pale blue (O), light purple (S), copper (U) and gold (Y)
- ½ yard each pale green (E), dark purple (Q), pale purple (T), light copper (V), dark orange (W) and orange (X)
- ⅝ yard each dark blue (L) and very dark purple (P)
- 1½ yards very dark blue (K)
- 3 yards medium blue (M)
- Backing 94" x 118"

- Batting 94" x 118"
- All-purpose thread to match fabrics
- Quilting thread
- Basic sewing tools and supplies

CUTTING

Step 1. Cut one 2½" by fabric width strip each fabrics B and H.

Step 2. Cut two 2½" by fabric width strips each fabrics A and G.

Step 3. Cut three 2½" by fabric width strips each fabrics F and Z.

Step 4. Cut four 2½" by fabric width strips each fabrics U and Y.

Step 5. Cut five 2½" by fabric width strips each fabrics V and X.

Step 6. Cut six 2½" by fabric width strips fabric W.

Step 7. Cut nine 2½" by fabric width strips fabric K for inner borders. Join strips on short ends to make one long strip; press seams open. Subcut

strip into two 96½" AA strips and two 76½" BB strips.

Step 8. Cut (10) 2½" by fabric width strips fabric M for binding.

Step 9. Cut one 3½" by fabric width strip each fabrics B, H, M and Q.

Step 10. Cut two 3½" by fabric width strips each fabrics C, I, N and R.

Step 11. Cut three 3½" by fabric width strips each fabrics D, J, O and S.

Step 12. Cut four 3½" by fabric width strips each fabrics E and T.

Step 13. Cut two 4½" by fabric width strips each fabrics Q and M.

Step 14. Cut four 4½" by fabric width strips each fabrics L and P.

Step 15. Cut six 4½" by fabric width strips fabric K.

Step 16. Cut (10) 6½" by fabric width strips fabric M for outside borders. Join strips on short ends to make one long strip; press seams open. Subcut strip into two 100½" CC and two 88½" DD strips.

PIECING THE PURPLE/BLUE IMPULSE BLOCKS

Step 1. Referring to Figure 1, sew Q to P to K with right sides together along length; press seams in one direction. Repeat for two strip sets. Repeat with P, K and L strips and K, L and M strips.

Figure 1

Step 2. Subcut the strip sets into (12) 4½" segments each referring to Figure 2.

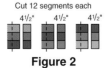

Figure 2

Step 3. Join one of each segment as shown in Figure 3 to complete one Purple/Blue Impulse

block; press seams in one direction. Repeat to make 12 blocks.

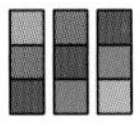

Figure 3

PIECING THE BLUE-GREEN IMPULSE BLOCKS

Step 1. Referring to Figure 4, sew B to C to D to E with right sides together along length; press seams in one direction. Repeat with C, D, E and O strips; D, E, O and N strips; and E, O, N and M strips.

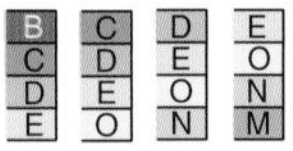

Figure 4

Step 2. Subcut the strip sets into (12) 3½" segments each referring to Figure 5.

Figure 5

Step 3. Join one of each segment as shown in Figure 6 to complete one Blue/Green Impulse block; press seams in one direction. Repeat to make 12 blocks.

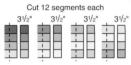

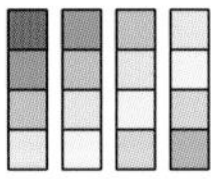

Figure 6

PIECING THE ORANGE/RED/GREEN IMPULSE BLOCKS

Step 1. Referring to Figure 7, sew W to X to Y to Z to A to B with right sides together along length; press seams in one direction. Repeat with V, W, X, Y, Z and A strips; U, V, W, X, Y and Z strips; F, U, V, W, X and Y strips; G, F, U, V, W and X strips; and H, G, F, U, V and W strips.

Figure 7

Step 2. Subcut the strip sets into (12) 2½" segments each referring to Figure 8.

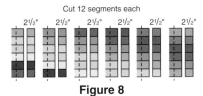

Cut 12 segments each

2½" 2½" 2½" 2½" 2½" 2½"

Figure 8

Step 3. Join one of each segment as shown in Figure 9 to complete one Orange/Red/Green Impulse block; press seams in one direction. Repeat to make 12 blocks.

Figure 9

PIECING THE RED/PURPLE IMPULSE BLOCKS

Step 1. Referring to Figure 10, sew T to J to I to H with right sides together along length; press seams in one direction. Repeat with S, T, J and I strips; R, S, T and J strips; and Q, R, S and T strips.

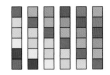

Figure 10

Step 2. Subcut the strip sets into (12) 3½" segments each referring to Figure 11.

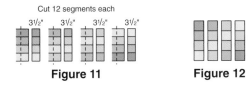

Cut 12 segments each

3½" 3½" 3½" 3½"

Figure 11   **Figure 12**

Step 3. Join one of each segment as shown in Figure 12 to complete one Red/Purple Impulse block; press seams in one direction. Repeat to make 12 blocks.

COMPLETING THE QUILT

Step 1. Arrange and join the blocks in rows referring to Figure 13; press seams in adjacent rows in opposite directions.

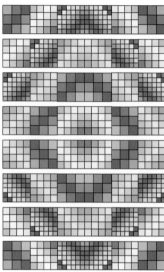

Figure 13

COLOR KEY

- Very dark green (A)
- Dark green (B)
- Medium green (C)
- Light green (D)
- Pale green (E)
- Very dark red (F)
- Dark red (G)
- Medium red (H)
- Light red (I)
- Pale red (J)
- Very dark blue (K)
- Dark blue (L)
- Medium blue (M)
- Light blue (N)
- Pale blue (O)
- Very dark purple (P)
- Dark purple (Q)
- Medium purple (R)
- Light purple (S)
- Pale purple (T)
- Copper (U)
- Light copper (V)
- Dark orange (W)
- Orange (X)
- Gold (Y)
- Light gold (Z)

Step 2. Sew an AA strip to opposite long sides and BB strips to the top and bottom of the pieced center; press seams toward the AA and BB strips.

Step 3. Sew CC strips to opposite long sides and DD strips to the top and bottom of the pieced center; press seams toward CC and DD strips.

Step 4. Complete the quilt using the previously cut binding strips and referring to Completing Your Quilt on page 170. ●

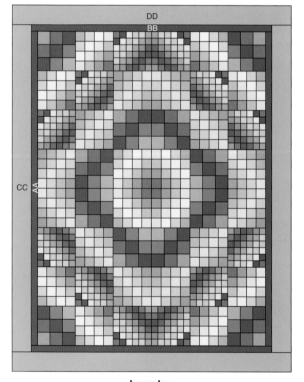

Impulse
Placement Diagram
88" x 112"

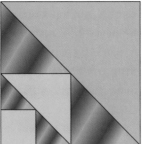

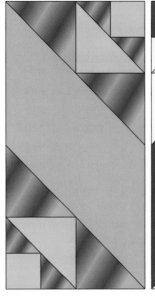

Purple Flying Goose
8" x 8" Block
Make 5

Pink Fying Goose
8" x 8" Block
Make 5

Pink Twister
8" x 16" Block
Make 25

Purple Twister
8" x 16" Block
Make 25

Tumbling Twister

A simple Flying Goose block is stretched to its limit to create the twisted ribbon design of this quilt.

PROJECT SPECIFICATIONS

Skill Level: Intermediate
Quilt Size: 95" x 103"
Block Size: 8" x 8" and 8" x 16"
Number of Blocks: 10 and 50

MATERIALS

All fabrics are batiks.

- ¾ yard rainbow mottled
- 1½ yards light salmon mottled
- 1¾ yards orange print
- 2¼ yards dark purple mottled
- 2⅝ yards bright pink mottled
- 3 yards multicolor metallic print
- Backing 101" x 109"
- Batting 101" x 109"
- Neutral color all-purpose thread
- Quilting thread
- Basic sewing tools and supplies

CUTTING

Step 1. Cut four 2½" by fabric width strips each dark purple mottled (A) and orange print (F); subcut strips into (55) 2½" squares each for A and F.

Step 2. Cut three 8⅞" x 8⅞" squares each dark purple (E) and bright pink (J) mottleds; cut each square in half on one diagonal to make six each E and J triangles. Discard one E and one J triangle.

Step 3. Cut nine 6⅛" by fabric width strips dark purple (K) and bright pink (L) mottleds. Unfold each strip, press flat and trim one end at a 45-degree angle as shown in Figure 1; cut three 8½" angled segments from each strip to total 25 each K and L pieces.

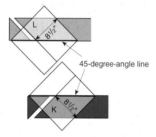

Figure 1

Step 4. Cut four 2⅞" by fabric width strips each light salmon mottled (B) and multicolor metallic print (G); subcut strips into (55) 2⅞" squares each fabric. Cut each square in half on one diagonal to make 110 each B and G triangles.

Step 5. Cut seven 4⅞" by fabric width strips each light salmon mottled (D) and multicolor metallic print (I); subcut strips into (55) 4⅞" squares each fabric. Cut each square in half on one diagonal to make 110 each D and I triangles.

Step 6. Cut four 4⅞" by fabric width strips each rainbow mottled (C) and orange print (H); subcut strips into (28) 4⅞" squares each. Cut each square in half on one diagonal to make 56 each C and H triangles; discard one C and one H triangle.

Step 7. Cut nine 2½" by fabric width strips orange print. Join strips on short ends to make one long strip; press seams open. Subcut strip into two 88½" L strips and two 84½" M strips.

Step 8. Cut four 6" x 6" P squares orange print.

Step 9. Cut nine 6" by fabric width strips multicolor metallic print. Join strips on short ends to make one long strip; press seams open. Subcut strip into two 92½" N strips and two 84½" O strips.

Step 10. Cut (10) 2¼" by fabric width strips bright pink mottled for binding.

PIECING THE PURPLE TWISTER BLOCKS

Step 1. To complete one Purple Twister block, sew B to two adjacent sides of A as shown in Figure 2; press seams toward B. Repeat to make two A-B units.

Figure 2

Step 2. Sew C to each A-B unit as shown in Figure 3; press seams toward C.

Figure 3

Step 3. Add D to two adjacent C sides of the A-B-C units to complete two purple corner units as shown in Figure 4; press seams toward D.

Figure 4

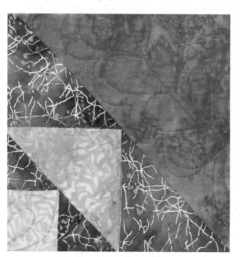

Step 4. Sew a purple corner unit to opposite angled ends of K to complete one Purple Twister block as shown in Figure 5; press seams toward K. Repeat to make 25 blocks.

Figure 5

PIECING THE PINK TWISTER BLOCKS

Step 1. Repeat Steps 1–3 for Piecing the Purple Twister Blocks using F, G, H and I pieces for corner units to make 50 pink corner units as shown in Figure 6.

Figure 6

Step 2. Sew a pink corner unit to opposite angled ends of L to complete one Pink Twister block as shown in Figure 7; press seams toward L. Repeat to make 25 blocks.

Figure 7

PIECING THE PURPLE FLYING GOOSE BLOCKS

Step 1. Repeat Steps 1–3 for Piecing the Purple Twister Blocks to make five purple corner units.
Step 2. Sew a purple corner unit to E to complete one block as shown in Figure 8; press seam toward E. Repeat to make five blocks.

Figure 8

PIECING THE PINK FLYING GOOSE BLOCKS

Step 1. Repeat Step 1 for Piecing the Pink Twister Blocks to make five pink corner units.
Step 2. Sew a pink corner unit to J to complete one block as shown in Figure 9; press seam toward J. Repeat to make five blocks.

Figure 9

COMPLETING THE QUILT

Step 1. Join five Purple Flying Goose blocks with five Pink Flying Goose blocks to make an X row as shown in Figure 10; press seams toward the Purple Flying Goose blocks.
Step 2. Join five Pink Twister blocks with five Purple Twister blocks to make a Y row, again referring to Figure 10; press seams toward the

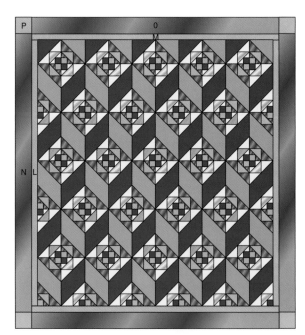

Tumbling Twister
Placement Diagram
95" x 103"

Purple Twister blocks. Repeat to make five Y rows.

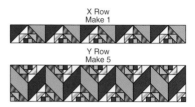

X Row
Make 1

Y Row
Make 5

Figure 10

Step 3. Join the rows beginning with the X row and referring to the Placement Diagram for positioning of the rows; press seams in one direction.

Step 4. Sew an L strip to opposite long sides and M strips to the top and bottom of the pieced center; press seams toward L and M strips.

Step 5. Sew an N strip to opposite sides of the pieced center; press seams toward N strips.

Step 6. Sew a P square to each end of each O strip; press seams toward O. Sew an O-P strip to the top and bottom of the pieced center to complete the pieced top; press seams toward the O-P strips.

Step 7. Complete the quilt using the previously cut binding strips and referring to Completing Your Quilt on page 170. ●

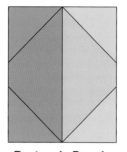
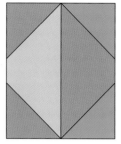
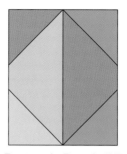
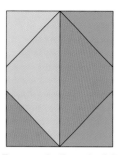

Rectangle Parade
7" x 8½" Block
Make 30

Rectangle Parade AA
7" x 8½" Block
Make 7

Rectangle Parade BB
7" x 8½" Block
Make 6

Rectangle Parade CC
7" x 8½" Block
Make 6

Rectangle Parade

Stretch a Snowball block, add a seam in the center and vary the colors in the corners, and you have a twist on a traditional quilt design.

PROJECT SPECIFICATIONS

Skill Level: Beginner
Quilt Size: 71" x 81"
Block Size: 7" x 8½"
Number of Blocks: 49

MATERIALS

All fabrics are batiks.

- 1 yard pink marbled
- 1¼ yards bright green waves
- 1¾ yards pink print
- 2⅜ yards blue print
- 2⅝ yards bright green swirls
- Backing 77" x 87"
- Batting 77" x 87"
- Neutral color all-purpose thread
- Quilting thread
- Basic sewing tools and supplies

CUTTING

Step 1. Cut five 9" by fabric width strips each bright green swirls (A) and blue print (B); subcut strips into 49 each 4" A and B rectangles.

Step 2. Cut four 6¼" by fabric width strips bright green swirls; subcut strips into (22) 6¼" squares. Cut each square on both diagonals to make 88 H triangles.

Step 3. Cut one 3⅜" by fabric width strip bright green swirls; subcut strip into eight 3⅜" squares. Cut each square in half on one diagonal to make 16 K triangles.

Step 4. Cut three 4" by fabric width strips blue

print; subcut strips into (26) 4" C squares. Draw a diagonal line from corner to corner on the wrong side of each square.

Step 5. Cut three 4¾" by fabric width strips each bright green swirls (I) and pink print (J); subcut strips into 24 each 4¾" squares. Cut each square in half on both diagonals to make 96 each I and J triangles.

Step 6. Cut (10) 3½" by fabric width strips pink print. Join strips on short ends to make one long strip; press seams open. Subcut the strip into two 60" F strips, two 75½" M strips and two 71½" N strips.

Step 7. Cut three 3¼" by fabric width strips pink print. Join strips on short ends to make one long strip; press seams open. Subcut the strip into two 55½" G strips.

Step 8. Cut one 5½" by fabric width strip blue print; subcut strip into four 5½" L squares.

Step 9. Cut (10) 4" by fabric width strips bright green waves; subcut strips into (98) 4" D squares. Draw a diagonal line from corner to corner on the wrong side of each square.

Step 10. Cut eight 4" by fabric width strips pink marbled; subcut strips into (72) 4" E squares. Draw a diagonal line from corner to corner on the wrong side of each square.

Step 11. Cut eight 2¼" by fabric width strips blue print for binding.

PIECING THE BLOCKS

Step 1. Referring to Figure 1, place a D square right sides together on one corner of B; stitch on the marked line. Trim seam to ¼"; press D to the right side. Repeat on the opposite end of B to complete a B-D unit. Repeat to make 49 B-D units.

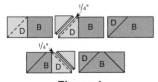

Figure 1

Step 2. Repeat Step 1 with A and C; A, C and E; and A and E to complete units referring to Figure 2.

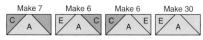

Figure 2

Step 3. To complete one Rectangle Parade block, join one B-D unit with one A-E unit as shown in Figure 3; press seams toward A-E. Repeat to make 30 blocks.

Figure 3

Step 4. Join units as shown in Figure 4 to complete seven AA blocks and six each BB and CC blocks; press seams toward A in all blocks.

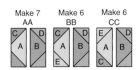

Figure 4

COMPLETING THE QUILT

Step 1. Join one AA and six CC blocks to make an X row as shown in Figure 5; press seams toward the AA block.

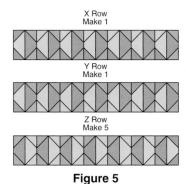

Figure 5

Step 2. Join one AA and six BB blocks to make a Y row, again referring to Figure 5; press seams toward the AA blocks.

Step 3. Join one AA and six Rectangle Parade blocks to make a Z row, again referring to Figure 5; press seams in one direction. Repeat to make five Z rows.

Step 4. Join the rows referring to the Placement Diagram for positioning; press seams in one direction.

Step 5. Sew an F strip to opposite long sides and G strips to the top and bottom of the pieced center; press seams toward F and G strips.

Step 6. Sew I to J to make a triangle unit as shown in Figure 6; press seam toward I. Repeat to make 96 triangle units.

Figure 6

Step 7. Join two triangle units to complete an I-J unit as shown in Figure 7; press seam in one direction. Repeat to make 48 I-J units.

Figure 7

Step 8. Sew H to the J sides of 20 I-J units to make the side units as shown in Figure 8; press seams toward H. Repeat to make 20 reverse side units, again referring to Figure 8.

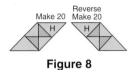

Figure 8

Step 9. Join nine side units as shown in Figure 9 to make the top row; press seams in one direction. Repeat with reverse side units for the bottom row, again referring to Figure 9.

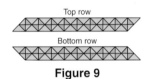

Figure 9

Step 10. Repeat Step 9 except use 11 side units to complete the left side row; press seams in one direction. Repeat with reverse side units to make the right side row.

Step 11. Sew H to one J side and K to the remaining J and one I side of an I-J unit to complete a corner unit as shown in Figure 10; press seams toward H and K. Repeat to make four corner units and four reverse corner units, again referring to Figure 10.

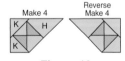

Figure 10

Step 12. Sew a corner unit to each end of the top row and the left side row referring to Figure 11; press seams in one direction. Repeat with the reverse corner units on the bottom and right side rows.

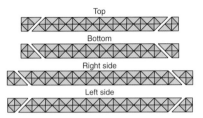

Figure 11

Sew 13. Sew the side rows to opposite long sides of the pieced center; press seams toward F strips.

Step 14. Sew an L square to each end of the top and bottom rows; press seams toward L.

Step 15. Sew the top row to the top and the bottom row to the bottom of the pieced center; press seams toward G strips.

Step 16. Sew M strips to opposite long sides and N strips to the top and bottom of the pieced center to complete the pieced top; press seams toward M and N strips.

Step 17. Complete the quilt using the previously cut binding strips and referring to Completing Your Quilt on page 170. ●

Rectangle Parade
Placement Diagram
71" x 81"

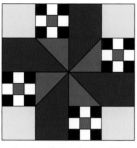

Lady of the Lake AA
12" x 12" Block
Make 2

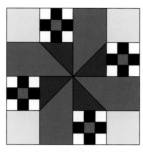

Lady of the Lake BB
12" x 12" Block
Make 2

Lady of the Lake CC
12" x 12" Block
Make 1

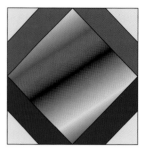

Friday the 13th
12" x 12" Block
Make 4

Ladies of the Lake

The traditional Lady of the Lake and Friday the 13th blocks combine to form a twisted design across the center of this wall quilt.

PROJECT SPECIFICATIONS

Skill Level: Intermediate
Quilt Size: 58" x 58"
Block Size: 12" x 12"
Number of Blocks: 9

MATERIALS

- ¼ yard red mottled
- ⅜ yard white tonal
- ½ yard light blue mottled
- 1 yard black mottled
- 1⅛ yards medium blue mottled
- 1⅛ yards dark blue mottled
- 1⅔ yards loon print
- Backing 64" x 64"
- Batting 64" x 64"
- Neutral color all-purpose thread
- Quilting thread
- Basic sewing tools and supplies

CUTTING

Step 1. Cut two 6½" x 46½" Q strips along the length of the loon print.

Step 2. Cut five 6½" by the remaining fabric width R strips loon print.

Step 3. Cut four 12½" x 12½" A squares loon print.

Step 4. Cut three 6½" by fabric width strips medium blue mottled; subcut strips into eight 6½" B squares and (10) 3½" E rectangles.

Step 5. Cut four 3½" by fabric width strips medium blue mottled; subcut strips into four 24" L strips and (14) 3½" K squares.

Step 6. Cut three 3½" by fabric width strips light

blue mottled; subcut strips into (36) 3½"
C squares.

Step 7. Cut three 6½" by fabric width strips
dark blue mottled; subcut strips into eight 6½"
D squares and (10) 3½" J rectangles.

Step 8. Cut four 3½" by fabric width strips dark
blue mottled; subcut strips into four 24" M strips
and (14) 3½" F squares.

Step 9. Cut three 1½" by fabric width G strips
red mottled. Cut one strip into two 21"-long half-
strips; cut two 1½" N squares from each half-strip.

Step 10. Cut six 1½" by fabric width H strips
white tonal; cut one strip into two 21"-long
half-strips.

Step 11. Cut six 1½" by fabric width I strips
black mottled; cut one strip into two 21"-long
half-strips.

Step 12. Cut five 1½" by fabric width strips black
mottled for O/P borders.

Step 13. Cut six 2¼" by fabric width strips black
mottled for binding.

PIECING THE FRIDAY THE 13TH BLOCKS

Step 1. Mark a diagonal line from corner to corner on the wrong side of each B and D square
and 16 C squares.

Step 2. Place a B square right sides together on
one corner of an A square as shown in Figure 1;
stitch on the marked line, trim seam allowance to
¼" and press B to the right side, again referring
to Figure 1.

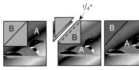

Figure 1

Step 3. Repeat with a second B square on an
adjacent corner of A and with D squares on the
remaining two corners of A as shown in Figure 2.

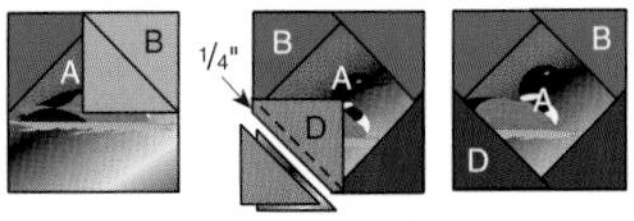

Figure 2

Step 4. Repeat with C squares on each corner of
the A-B-D unit to complete one Friday the 13th
block as shown in Figure 3; repeat to complete
four blocks, again referring to Figure 3 for positioning of B and D. **Note:** *The A squares in the
sample were cut from a directional print, making
it necessary to place the B and D squares on
different corners from block to block to keep the
print upright in the finished quilt. If your fabric is
not directional, all the squares can be stitched on
the same corners for all the blocks as shown in
the block drawing.*

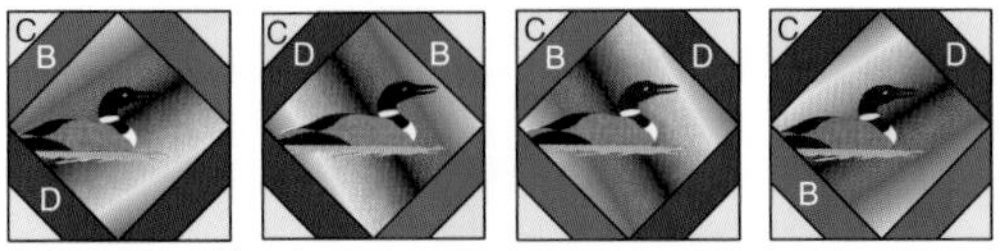

Figure 3

PIECING THE LADY OF THE LAKE BLOCKS

Step 1. Sew an I strip between two H strips with
right sides together along length to make a strip
set; press seams toward I.

Step 2. Cut the strip set into (20) 1½" W units as
shown in Figure 4.

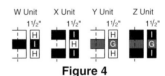

Figure 4

Step 3. Sew an H strip between two I strips with
right sides together along length to make a strip
set; press seams toward I.

Step 4. Cut the strip set into (20) 1½" X units,
again referring to Figure 4.

Step 5. Sew a G strip between two H strips with
right sides together along length to make a strip
set; press seams toward G. Repeat with G and H
half-strips to make a half-strip set.

Step 6. Cut the strip sets into (38) 1½" Y units,
again referring to Figure 4; set aside 28 units for
the pieced border.

Step 7. Sew a G strip between two I strips with

right sides together along length to make a strip set; press seams toward I. Repeat with G and I half-strips to make a half-strip set.

Step 8. Cut the strip sets into (38) 1½" Z units, again referring to Figure 4; set aside 28 units for the pieced border.

Step 9. Sew a Y unit between two X units to make an X-Y unit as shown in Figure 5; press seams toward the X units. Repeat to make 10 X-Y units.

Figure 5   **Figure 6**

Step 10. Sew a Z unit between two W units to make a W-Z unit, again referring to Figure 5; press seams toward the Z unit. Repeat to make 10 W-Z units.

Step 11. Sew a C square to each X-Y unit and each W-Z unit to make 10 each C-X-Y units and C-W-Z units as shown in Figure 6; press seams toward C.

Step 12. Mark a diagonal line from corner to corner on the wrong side of each F and K square.

Step 13. Place an F square right sides together on one end of E as shown in Figure 7; stitch, trim and press F to the right side to complete one E-F unit, again referring to Figure 7. Repeat to make 10 E-F units.

Figure 7

Step 14. Repeat Step 13 with K squares and J rectangles to make 10 J-K units, again referring to Figure 7.

Step 15. Sew a J-K unit to each C-X-Y unit to make 10 dark quarter-block units as shown in Figure 8; press seams toward J-K. Repeat with E-F and C-W-Z units to make 10 medium quarter-block units, again referring to Figure 8; press seams toward E-F.

Figure 8   **Figure 9**

Step 16. Join four dark quarter-block units to make a Lady of the Lake AA block referring to Figure 9 and the block drawing; press seams in one direction. Repeat to make two blocks.

Step 17. Join four medium quarter-block units to make a Lady of the Lake BB block referring to the block drawing; press seams in one direction. Repeat to make two blocks.

Step 18. Join two each medium and dark quarter-block units to make the Lady of the Lake CC block referring to the block drawing; press seams in one direction.

COMPLETING THE QUILT

Step 1. Join three blocks to make a row referring to the Placement Diagram for positioning of blocks; press seams in one direction. Repeat to make three rows, pressing seams in opposite directions from row to row.

Step 2. Join the rows to complete the pieced center; press seams in one direction.

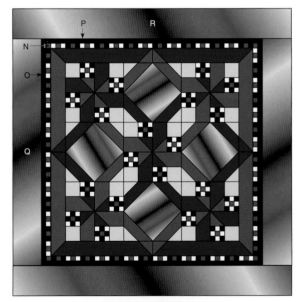

Ladies of the Lake
Placement Diagram
58" x 58"

Step 3. Place an F square right sides together on one end of an L strip; stitch, trim and press F to the right side to complete one F-L strip as shown in Figure 10; repeat to make two F-L and two reversed F-L strips, again referring to Figure 10.

Step 4. Repeat Step 3 with K squares and M strips to make two each K-M and reversed K-M strips, again referring to Figure 10.

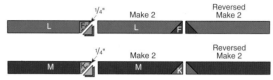

Figure 10

Step 5. Join an F-L strip and a reversed F-L strip as shown in Figure 11; press seam in one direction. Repeat for two pieced strips.

Figure 11

Step 6. Center and sew a pieced strip to opposite sides of the pieced center, stopping stitching ¼" from each corner.

Step 7. Repeat Steps 5 and 6 with K-M and reversed K-M strips to make two pieced strips and stitch to the top and bottom of the pieced center.

Step 8. Miter corners; trim seam to ¼". Press corner seams open and border seams toward the pieced strips.

Step 9. Join seven each Y and Z units on short ends to make a border strip as shown in Figure 12; press seams toward the Z units. Repeat to make four strips.

Figure 12

Step 10. Sew a strip to opposite sides of the pieced center referring to the Placement Diagram for positioning of strips; press seams away from the strips.

Step 11. Sew an N square to each end of the remaining Y-Z strips; press seams toward N. Sew a strip to the top and bottom of the pieced center; press seams away from the strips.

Step 12. Join the O/P strips on short ends to make a long strip; press seams in one direction. Cut into two 44½" O strips and two 46½" P strips.

Step 13. Sew the O strips to opposite sides and the P strips to the top and bottom of the pieced center; press seams toward the O and P strips.

Step 14. Sew the Q strips to opposite sides of the pieced center; press seams toward the Q strips.

Step 15. Join the R strips on short ends to make a long strip; press seams in one direction. Cut into two 58½" R strips.

Step 16. Sew the R strips to the top and bottom of the pieced center; press seams toward the R strips to complete the top.

Step 17. Complete the quilt using the previously cut binding strips and referring to Completing Your Quilt on page 170. ●

design by **LINDA MILLER**

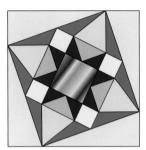

Dogtooth Violet
10¾" x 10¾" Block
Make 13

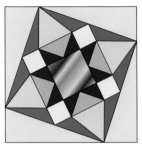

Reversed Dogtooth Violet
10¾" x 10¾" Block
Make 12

Diamond Twist

Give your blocks a twist, add angled pieces and the result is a quilt design that dances across the rows.

PROJECT SPECIFICATIONS
Skill Level: Intermediate
Quilt Size: 69¾" x 69¾"
Block Size: 10¾" x 10¾"
Number of Blocks: 25

MATERIALS
All fabrics are batiks.
- ½ yard cream multicolor
- ⅝ yard blue
- ¾ yard dark teal
- ⅞ yard light lavender
- 1 yard light teal
- 1 yard dark purple
- 1⅜ yards light turquoise/lavender
- 1⅝ yards blue multicolor
- Backing 76" x 76"
- Batting 76" x 76"
- Neutral color all-purpose thread
- Quilting thread
- Basic sewing tools and supplies

CUTTING
Step 1. Prepare templates using pattern pieces given; cut as directed on each piece.

Step 2. Cut three 3½" by fabric width strips blue multicolor; subcut strips into (25) 3½" B squares.

Step 3. Cut seven 6" by fabric width strips blue multicolor. Join strips on short ends to make one long strip; press seams open. Subcut strip into two 59¼" L and two 70¼" M strips.

Step 4. Cut five 2" by fabric width strips cream multicolor; subcut strips into (100) 2" C squares.

Step 5. Cut five 3½" by fabric width strips light lavender; subcut strips into (100) 2" D rectangles.

Step 6. Cut six 1½" by fabric width strips light lavender. Join strips on short ends to make one long strip; press seams open. Subcut strip into two 54¼" H strips and two 56¼" I strips.

Step 7. Cut (10) 2" by fabric width strips dark purple; subcut strips into (200) E squares. Draw a diagonal line from corner to corner on the wrong side of each square.

Step 8. Cut six 2" by fabric width strips dark purple. Join strips on short ends to make one long

Step 3. To complete one block unit, sew a D-E unit to opposite sides of B as shown in Figure 3; press seams toward B.

Figure 3   **Figure 4**

Step 4. Sew C to each end of a D-E unit to make a side unit as shown in Figure 4; press seams toward C. Repeat to make two side units.

Step 5. Sew a side unit to opposite sides of the B-D-E unit as shown in Figure 5; press seams toward the B-D-E unit.

Figure 5   **Figure 6**

Step 6. Sew an A-F unit to each side of the pieced unit to complete a block unit as shown in Figure 6; press seams toward the A-F units. Repeat to make 25 block units.

Step 7. Sew G to each side of 13 block units to complete one Dogtooth Violet block as shown

strip; press seams open. Subcut strip into two 56¼" J strips and two 59¼" K strips.

Step 9. Cut seven 2¼" by fabric width strips blue for binding.

PIECING THE BLOCKS

Step 1. Referring to Figure 1, place E right sides together on one end of D; stitch on the marked line. Trim seam allowance to ¼"; press E to the right side. Repeat on the opposite end of D to complete a D-E unit. Repeat to make 100 D-E units.

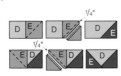

Figure 1

Step 2. Sew A and AR to the long sides of F to make an A-F unit as shown in Figure 2; press seams toward A. Repeat to make 100 A-F units.

Figure 2

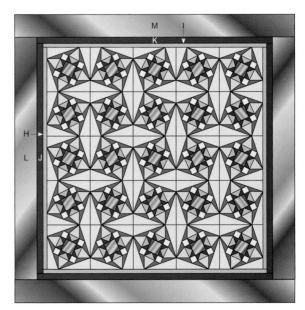

Diamond Twist
Placement Diagram
69¾" x 69¾"

in Figure 7. Repeat with GR on the remaining 12 block units to complete Reversed Dogtooth Violet blocks. Press seams toward G or GR.

Figure 7

COMPLETING THE QUILT

Step 1. Join three Dogtooth Violet blocks with two Reversed Dogtooth Violet blocks to make an X row referring to Figure 8; press seams in one direction. Repeat to make three X rows.

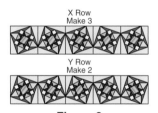

Figure 8

Step 2. Join three Reversed Dogtooth Violet blocks with two Dogtooth Violet blocks to make a Y row, again referring to Figure 8; press seams in the opposite direction from the X rows. Repeat to make two Y rows.

Step 3. Join the rows referring to the Placement Diagram for positioning; press seams in one direction.

Step 4. Sew H strips to opposite sides and I strips to the top and bottom of the pieced center; press seams toward H and I strips.

Step 5. Sew J strips to opposite sides and K strips to the top and bottom of the pieced center; press seams toward J and K strips.

Step 6. Sew L strips to opposite sides and M strips to the top and bottom of the pieced center; press seams toward L and M strips.

Step 7. Complete the quilt using the previously cut binding strips and referring to Completing Your Quilt on page 170. ●

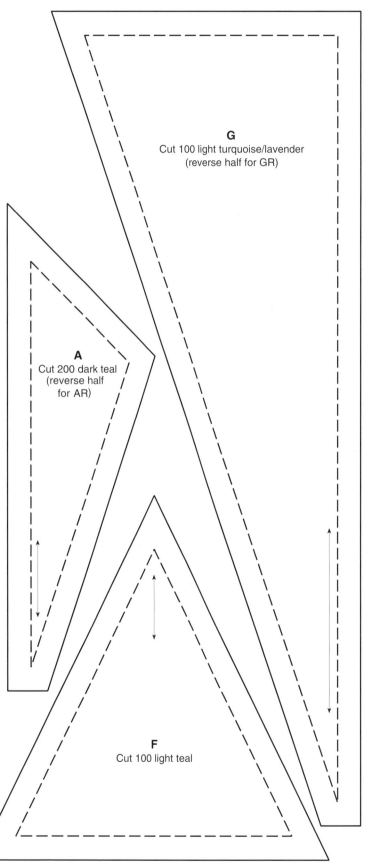

G
Cut 100 light turquoise/lavender
(reverse half for GR)

A
Cut 200 dark teal
(reverse half
for AR)

F
Cut 100 light teal

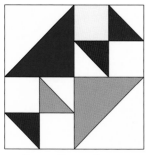

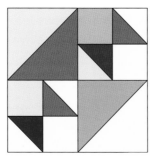

Green Fox & Geese
6" x 6" Block
Make 16

Red Fox & Geese
6" x 6" Block
Make 16

Solitude Medallion

Four Fox & Geese blocks set together in pairs of matching colors or alternating colors create a secondary X & O design in this scrappy queen-size quilt.

PROJECT SPECIFICATIONS

Skill Level: Intermediate
Quilt Size: 94" x 94"
Block Size: 6" x 6"
Number of Blocks: 32

MATERIALS

- 1 (4½" x 4½") square each 4 different tan-with-red prints (M)
- ½ yard total red scraps
- ⅔ yard total green scraps
- 1½ yards red print
- 1¾ yards green star print
- 2½ yards green leaf print
- 3¼ yards total cream and tan scraps
- Backing 100" x 100"
- Batting 100" x 100"

- Neutral color all-purpose thread
- Quilting thread
- Basic sewing tools and supplies

CUTTING

Step 1. Cut (36) 3⅞" x 3⅞" squares cream/tan scraps; cut each square in half on one diagonal to make 72 A triangles.

Step 2. Cut (64) 2⅜" x 2⅜" squares cream/tan scraps; cut each square in half on one diagonal to make 128 C triangles.

Step 3. Cut (128) 2" x 2" E squares cream/tan scraps.

Step 4. Cut eight 3½" x 21½" J strips cream/tan scraps.

Step 5. Cut four 12½" x 12½" H squares cream/tan scraps.

Step 6. Cut eight 6½" x 12½" I strips cream/tan scraps.

Step 7. Cut (20) 3⅞" x 3⅞" squares red scraps; cut each square in half on one diagonal to make 40 B triangles.

Step 8. Cut (32) 2⅜" x 2⅜" squares red scraps; cut each square in half on one diagonal to make 64 D triangles.

Step 9. Cut (16) 3⅞" x 3⅞" squares green scraps; cut each square in half on one diagonal to make 32 F triangles.

Step 10. Cut (32) 2⅜" x 2⅜" squares green scraps; cut each square in half on one diagonal to make 64 G triangles.

Step 11. Cut four 3½" x 3½" K squares green scraps.

Step 12. Cut six 4½" by fabric width strips red print. Join strips on short ends to make one long strip; press seams open. Subcut strip into four 54½" L strips.

Step 13. Cut (10) 2¼" by fabric width strips red print for binding.

Step 14. Cut two 10½" x 62½" N strips and two 10½" x 82½" O strips along the length of the green leaf print.

Step 15. Cut nine 6½" by fabric width strips green star print. Join strips on short ends to make one long strip; press seams open. Subcut strip into two 82½" P strips and two 94½" Q strips.

PIECING THE RED FOX & GEESE BLOCKS

Step 1. To piece one Red Fox & Geese block, sew C to D to complete a C-D unit as shown in Figure 1; press seam toward D. Repeat to make four C-D units.

Figure 1

Step 2. Sew E to a C-D unit as shown in Figure 2; repeat to make four C-D-E units. Press seam toward E.

Figure 2

Step 3. Join two C-D-E units to complete a corner unit as shown in Figure 3; press seam in one direction. Repeat to make two corner units.

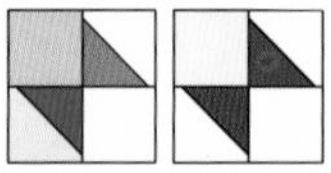

Figure 3

Step 4. Sew A to B to complete an A-B unit as shown in Figure 4; press seam toward B. Repeat to make two A-B units.

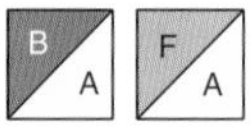

Figure 4

Step 5. Sew an A-B unit to a corner unit to make a row as shown in Figure 5; press seam toward the A-B unit. Repeat to make two rows.

Figure 5

Step 6. Join the rows referring to Figure 6 to complete one Red Fox & Geese block; press seam in one direction. Repeat to make 16 blocks.

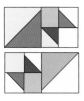

Figure 6

PIECING THE GREEN FOX & GEESE BLOCKS

Step 1. To piece one Green Fox & Geese block, sew C to G to complete a C-G unit as shown in Figure 1; press seam toward G. Repeat to make four C-G units.

Step 2. Sew E to a C-G unit as shown in Figure 2; repeat to make four C-G-E units. Press seam toward E.

Step 3. Join two C-G-E units to complete a corner unit as shown in Figure 3; press seam in one direction. Repeat to make two corner units.

Step 4. Sew A to F to complete an A-F unit as shown in Figure 4; press seam toward F. Repeat to make two A-F units.

Step 5. Sew an A-F unit to a corner unit to make a row as shown in Figure 7; press seam toward the A-F unit. Repeat to make two rows.

Figure 7

Step 6. Join the rows referring to Figure 8 to complete one Green Fox & Geese block; press seam in one direction. Repeat to make 16 blocks.

Figure 8

COMPLETING THE QUILT

Step 1. Join two Green Fox & Geese blocks with two Red Fox & Geese blocks and two I pieces to complete an X row referring to Figure 9; press seams toward I. Repeat to make two X rows.

X Row

Figure 9

Step 2. Join two Green Fox & Geese blocks with two Red Fox & Geese blocks to make a red/green block unit as shown in Figure 10; repeat to make four red/green block units. Press seams toward the Green Fox & Geese blocks and in one direction.

Figure 10

Step 3. Join two red/green block units with two I pieces and one H square to make a Y row as shown in Figure 11; press seams toward I and H. Repeat to make two Y rows.

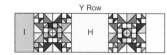

Y Row

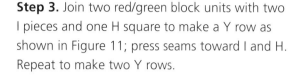

Figure 11

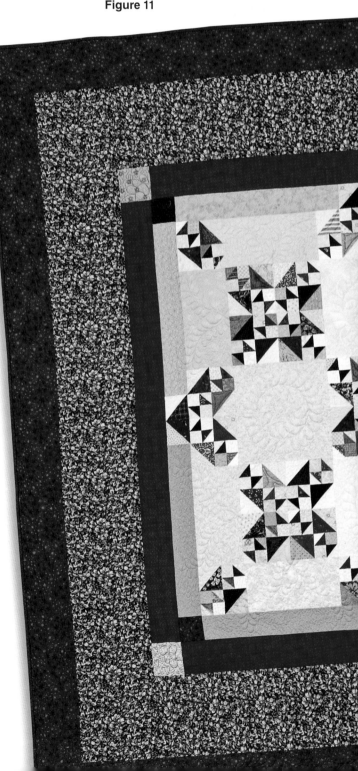

Step 4. Join four Green Fox & Geese blocks to make a green block unit as shown in Figure 12; press seams in opposite directions in the rows and in one direction in the unit.

Figure 12

Step 5. Join two Red Fox & Geese blocks to make a red half-unit as shown in Figure 13; press seams in one direction. Repeat to make two red half-units.

Figure 13

Step 6. Join two H squares with the green block unit and the two red half-units to complete the Z row as shown in Figure 14; press seams toward H.

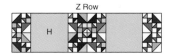

Figure 14

Step 7. Join the X, Y and Z rows referring to the Placement Diagram to complete the pieced center; press seams in one direction.

Step 8. Sew A to B to complete an A-B unit, again referring to Figure 4; press seam toward B. Repeat to make eight A-B units.

Step 9. Join two A-B units as shown in Figure 15 to make a side unit; press seams in one direction. Repeat to make four side units.

Figure 15

Step 10. Sew a J strip to opposite ends of each side unit; press seams toward J. Sew a J-side unit to opposite sides of the pieced center referring to the Placement Diagram for positioning; press seams toward J-side units.

Step 11. Sew a K square to each end of each remaining J-side unit; press seams away from K. Sew these strips to the top and bottom of the pieced center, again referring to the Placement Diagram for positioning.

Step 12. Sew an L strip to opposite sides of the pieced center; press seams toward L strips.

Step 13. Sew an M square to each end of the remaining L strips; press seams toward L strips. Sew these strips to the top and bottom of the pieced center; press seams toward L-M strips.

Step 14. Sew an N strip to opposite sides and O strips to the top and bottom of the pieced center; press seams toward N and O strips.

Step 15. Sew a P strip to opposite sides and Q strips to the top and bottom of the pieced center to complete the pieced top; press seams toward P and Q strips.

Step 16. Complete the quilt using the previously cut binding strips and referring to Completing Your Quilt on page 170. ●

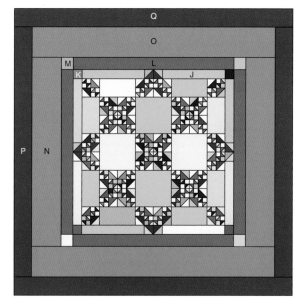

Solitude Medallion
Placement Diagram
94" x 94"

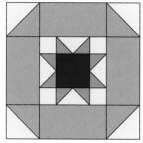

Pieced Star Variation
12" x 12" Block
Make 18

Sawtooth/Churn Dash
12" x 12" Block
Make 17

Star to Star

The Pieced Star Variation block forms the large star in this quilt, while the second block contains a tiny Sawtooth Star nestled in a Churn Dash block.

PROJECT SPECIFICATIONS
Skill Level: Intermediate
Quilt Size: 84" x 108"
Block Size: 12" x 12"
Number of Blocks: 35

MATERIALS
- ¾ yard green print
- 1 yard purple print
- 1¼ yards magenta mottled
- 2 yards cream mottled
- 2¼ yards gold print
- 5½ yards large floral
- Backing 90" x 114"
- Batting 90" x 114"
- Neutral color all-purpose thread
- Quilting thread
- Basic sewing tools and supplies

CUTTING
Step 1. Cut (12) 6½" by fabric width strips large floral; subcut strips into (140) 3½" A rectangles.

Step 2. Cut four 3⅞" by fabric width strips large floral; subcut strips into (34) 3⅞" squares. Cut each square in half on one diagonal to make 68 B triangles.

Step 3. Cut two strips each 8" x 93½" for L and 8" x 84½" for M along the remaining length of large floral.

Step 4. Cut four 3⅞" by fabric width strips cream mottled; subcut strips into (34) 3⅞" squares. Cut each square in half on one diagonal to make 68 C triangles.

Step 5. Cut six 3½" by fabric width E strips cream mottled; subcut four strips into (68) 2" E rectangles. Set aside remaining strips for E-I strip sets.

Step 6. Cut (15) 2" by fabric width G strips cream mottled; subcut four strips into (68) 2" G squares. Set aside remaining strips for D-G and G-I strip sets.

Step 7. Cut nine 3½" by fabric width D strips purple print; subcut two strips into (17) 3½" D squares. Set aside remaining strips for D-G and D-H strip sets.

Step 8. Cut seven 2" by fabric width strips gold print; subcut strips into (136) 2" F squares.

Step 9. Cut (17) 3½" by fabric width strips gold print; subcut 12 strips into (144) 3½" H squares. Set aside remaining strips for D-H strip sets.

Step 10. Cut (11) 2" by fabric width I strips magenta mottled.

Step 11. Cut eight 2" by fabric width strips magenta mottled for J/K borders.

Step 12. Cut (10) 2¼" by fabric width strips green print for binding.

PIECING THE SAWTOOTH/CHURN DASH BLOCKS

Step 1. Sew a B triangle to a C triangle along the diagonal as shown in Figure 1; press seams toward B. Repeat to make 68 B-C units.

Figure 1

Step 2. Mark a diagonal line from corner to corner on the wrong side of each F square.

Step 3. Place an F square right sides together on one end of E as shown in Figure 2; stitch on the marked line, trim seam allowance to ¼" and press F to the right side, again referring to Figure 2. Repeat on the remaining end of E to complete one E-F unit, again referring to Figure 2; repeat to make 68 E-F units.

Figure 2   **Figure 3**

Step 4. To piece one block, sew an E-F unit to opposite sides of a D square as shown in Figure 3; press seams toward D.

Step 5. Sew a G square to each end of an E-F

unit, again referring to Figure 3; press seams toward G. Repeat for two pieced strips.

Step 6. Sew a pieced strip to the remaining sides of the D square to complete the center unit, again referring to Figure 3; press seams toward the center unit.

Step 7. Sew an A rectangle to opposite sides of the center unit to complete the block center row referring to Figure 4; press seams toward A.

Figure 4

Step 8. Sew a B-C unit to each end of two A rectangles to complete the block top and bottom rows, again referring to Figure 4 for positioning; press seams toward A.

Step 9. Sew the block center row between the block top and bottom rows to complete one Sawtooth/Churn Dash block; press seams away from the center row. Repeat to make 17 blocks.

PIECING THE PIECED STAR VARIATION BLOCKS

Step 1. Sew a D strip between two G strips with right sides together along length; press seams toward D. Repeat to make two strip sets.

Step 2. Cut the strip sets into (18) 3½" D-G units as shown in Figure 5.

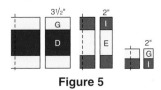

Figure 5

Step 3. Sew an E strip between two I strips with right sides together along length to make a strip set; press seams toward I. Repeat to make two strip sets.

Step 4. Cut the strip sets into (36) 2" E-I units, again referring to Figure 5.

Step 5. Sew a G strip to an I strip with right sides together along length to make a strip set; press seam toward I. Repeat to make seven strip sets.

Step 6. Cut the strip sets into (144) 2" G-I units, again referring to Figure 5.

Step 7. Join two G-I units to make a Four-Patch unit as shown in Figure 6; press seam to one side. Repeat to make 72 Four-Patch units.

Step 8. Mark a diagonal line from corner to corner on the wrong side of each H square.

Step 9. Using H squares and A rectangles, complete 72 A-H units as for the E-F units and referring to Figure 7.

Figure 6   **Figure 7**

Step 10. To piece one block, sew an E-I unit to opposite sides of a D-G unit to complete the center unit as shown in Figure 8; press seams toward D-G.

Figure 8

Step 11. Sew an A-H unit to opposite sides of the center unit to complete the block center row referring to Figure 9; press seams toward the center unit.

Figure 9

Step 12. Sew a Four-Patch unit to each end of two A-H units to make the block top and bottom rows, again referring to Figure 9; press seams toward the Four-Patch units.

Step 13. Sew the block center row between the block top and bottom rows to complete one Pieced Star Variation block; press seams toward the center row. Repeat to make 18 blocks.

COMPLETING THE QUILT

Step 1. Join three Pieced Star Variation blocks with two Sawtooth/Churn Dash blocks to make a row as shown in Figure 10; press seams toward the Sawtooth/Churn Dash blocks. Repeat to make four rows.

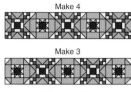
Make 4

Make 3

Figure 10

Step 2. Join three Sawtooth/Churn Dash blocks with two Pieced Star Variation blocks to make a row, again referring to Figure 10; press seams toward the Sawtooth/Churn Dash blocks. Repeat to make three rows.

Step 3. Join the rows to complete the pieced center referring to the Placement Diagram for positioning of rows; press seams in one direction.

Step 4. Join the J/K border strips on short ends to make a long strip; press seams to one side. Cut into two 84½" J strips and two 63½" K strips.

Step 5. Sew the J strips to opposite long sides and the K strips to the top and bottom of the pieced center; press seams toward strips.

Step 6. Sew a D strip to an H strip with right sides together along length to make a strip set; press seam toward D. Repeat to make five strip sets.

Step 7. Cut the strip sets into (52) 3½" D-H units as shown in Figure 11.

3½"
H
D

Figure 11

Step 8. Join 15 D-H units to make a strip; press seams in one direction. Repeat for two strips. Remove the purple D square from one end of each strip as shown in Figure 12; set aside.

Remove
D
Make 2

Figure 12

Step 9. Sew a pieced strip to opposite sides of the pieced center; press seams toward J strips.

Step 10. Join 11 D-H units to make a strip; repeat for two strips. Add a purple D square to the gold end of each strip as shown in Figure 13; press seams in one direction.

Add
D
Make 2

Figure 13

Step 11. Sew a pieced strip to the top and bottom of the pieced center; press seams toward K strips.

Step 12. Sew L strips to opposite long sides and M strips to the top and bottom of the pieced center; press seams toward strips to complete the top.

Step 13. Complete the quilt using the previously cut binding strips and referring to Completing Your Quilt on page 170. ●

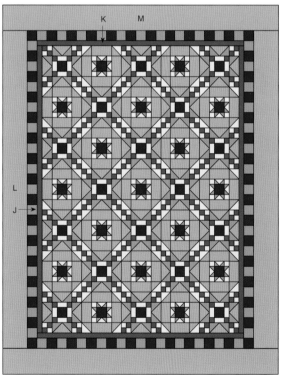
Star to Star
Placement Diagram
84" x 108"

design by **JULIE WEAVER**

Small Ohio Star Variation
12" x 12" Block
Make 15

Large Ohio Star Variation
12" x 12" Block
Make 15

Stars Above

Variations of the Ohio Star block come together, without the aid of sashing, to create the diagonal lines of this quilt. Study it and all sorts of patterns emerge.

PROJECT SPECIFICATIONS
Skill Level: Intermediate
Quilt Size: 88" x 100"
Block Size: 12" x 12"
Number of Blocks: 30

MATERIALS
- ⅛ yard green print
- ⅓ yard gold print
- 1⅝ yards red tonal
- 2⅝ yards small navy floral
- 3¾ yards large navy floral
- 4½ yards cream tonal
- Backing 94" x 106"
- Batting 94" x 106"
- Neutral color all-purpose thread
- Quilting thread
- Basic sewing tools and supplies

CUTTING
Step 1. Cut nine 4½" by fabric width strips small navy floral; subcut strips into (75) 4½" A squares.

Step 2. Cut (16) 1½" by fabric width strips small navy floral. Join strips on short ends to make one long strip; press seams open. Subcut strips into two strips each 72½" O, 62½" P, 98½" W and 88½" X.

Step 3. Cut (10) 2¼" by fabric width strips small navy floral for binding.

Step 4. Cut eight 2½" by fabric width strips cream tonal; subcut strips into (120) 2½" squares. Draw a diagonal line from corner to corner on the wrong side of 60 squares for B; set aside remaining squares for K.

Step 5. Cut two 5¼" by fabric width strips cream tonal; subcut strips into (15) 5¼" C squares. Draw a diagonal line from corner to corner on the wrong side of each square.

Step 6. Cut (12) 4" by fabric width strips cream tonal: subcut strips into (120) 4" F squares. Draw a diagonal line from corner to corner on the wrong side of each square.

Step 7. Cut two 3¼" by fabric width strips cream tonal; subcut strips into (15) 3¼" J squares. Draw a diagonal line from corner to corner on the wrong side of each square.

Step 8. Cut four 5⅛" strips cream tonal; subcut strips into (30) 5⅛" L squares. Cut each square in half on one diagonal to make 60 L triangles.

Step 9. Cut seven 4½" by fabric width strips cream tonal; subcut strips into (60) 4½" N squares. Draw a diagonal line from corner to corner on the wrong side of each square.

Step 10. Cut seven 2" by fabric width strips cream tonal. Join strips on short ends to make one long strip; press seams open. Subcut strip into two 74½" R strips and two 62½" S strips.

Step 11. Cut four 5¼" by fabric width strips red tonal; subcut strips into (30) 5¼" D squares.

Step 12. Cut three 3¼" by fabric width strips red tonal; subcut strips into (30) 3¼" I squares.

Step 13. Cut two 11" by fabric width strips red tonal; subcut strips into four 11" T squares and four 1½" x 1½" Q squares.

Step 14. Cut two 5¼" by fabric width strips large navy floral; subcut strips into (15) 5¼" E squares. Draw a line from corner to corner on the wrong side of each square.

Step 15. Cut five 6⅞" by fabric width strips large navy floral; subcut strips into (30) 6⅞" M squares.

Step 16. Cut seven 11" by fabric width strips large navy floral. Join strips on short ends to make one long strip; press seams open. Subcut strip into two 77½" U strips and two 65½" V strips.

Step 17. Cut one 2½" by fabric width strip green print; subcut strip into (15) 2½" G squares.

Step 18. Cut two 3¼" by fabric width strips gold print; subcut strips into (15) 3¼" H squares. Draw a diagonal line from corner to corner on the wrong side of each square.

PIECING THE LARGE OHIO STAR VARIATION BLOCKS

Step 1. Place an E square right sides together with a D square. Stitch ¼" on each side of the marked line and cut apart on the marked line as shown in Figure 1. Press seams toward E to make two D-E units. Repeat to make 30 D-E units.

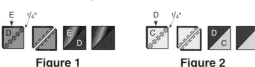

Figure 1   **Figure 2**

Step 2. Repeat Step 1 to complete (30) C-D units referring to Figure 2; press seams toward D.

Step 3. With right sides together, place a D-E unit on a C-D unit; draw a diagonal line on the unstitched diagonal of one of the units as shown in Figure 3.

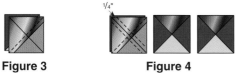

Figure 3   **Figure 4**

Step 4. Referring to Figure 4, stitch ¼" on each side of the marked line; cut apart on the marked line. Open and press seams toward the D-E units to make a side unit. Repeat to make 60 side units.

Step 5. Select 15 A squares; set aside remaining squares for A-F units. Referring to Figure 5, pin B right sides together on opposite corners of A; stitch on the marked lines. Trim seams to ¼"; press B to the right side.

Figure 5   **Figure 6**

Step 6. Repeat Step 5 on the remaining corners of A to complete 15 center units as shown in Figure 6.

Step 7. Referring to Figure 7, place an F square on one corner of one of the remaining A squares; stitch on the marked line. Trim seam to ¼"; press F to the right side.

Figure 7

Step 8. Repeat Step 7 on the opposite corner of A to complete a corner unit, again referring to Figure 7. Repeat to make 60 corner units.

Step 9. To complete one Large Ohio Star Variation block, sew a side unit to opposite sides of a center unit to make the center row referring to Figure 8; press seams toward the side units.

Step 10. Sew a corner unit to opposite sides of a side unit to make the top row, again referring to Figure 8; press seams toward the side unit. Repeat to make the bottom row.

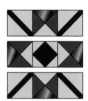

Figure 8

Step 11. Join the rows to complete one block; press seams away from the center row. Repeat to make 15 blocks.

PIECING THE SMALL OHIO STAR VARIATION BLOCKS

Step 1. Place an H square right sides together with an I square. Stitch ¼" on each side of the marked line and cut apart on the marked line as shown in Figure 9; press seam toward I. Repeat to make 30 H-I units.

Figure 9   **Figure 10**

Step 2. Repeat Step 1 to complete 30 I-J units referring to Figure 10; press seams toward I.

Step 3. With right sides together, place an H-I unit on an I-J unit; draw a diagonal line on the unstitched diagonal of one of the units as shown in Figure 11.

Figure 11

Step 4. Referring to Figure 12, stitch ¼" on each side of the marked line; cut apart on the marked line. Open and press seams toward the H-I units to make a side unit. Repeat to make 60 side units.

Figure 12   **Figure 13**

Step 5. Sew a side unit to opposite sides of G to make a G row as shown in Figure 13; press seams toward G.

Step 6. Sew K to the I sides of a side unit to make a K row, again referring to Figure 13; press seams toward K. Repeat to make a second K row.

Step 7. Sew a K row to opposite sides of the G row to complete a block center, again referring to Figure 13; press seams toward the K rows. Repeat to make 15 block centers.

Step 8. Sew L to each side of each block center as shown in Figure 14; press seams toward L.

Figure 14

Step 9. With right sides together, place an N square on the upper right and lower left corners of an M square as shown in Figure 15; stitch on the marked lines.

Step 10. Trim seam to ¼"; press N to the right side, again referring to Figure 15. Repeat to make 30 M-N units.

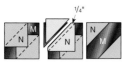

Figure 15

Figure 16

Step 11. Cut each M-N unit in half in the center of M as shown in Figure 16 to make 60 corner units.

Step 12. Sew a corner unit to each side of a completed L-block center unit to complete one Small Ohio Star Variation block as shown in Figure 17; repeat to make 15 blocks.

Figure 17

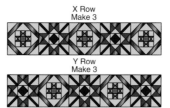

X Row
Make 3

Y Row
Make 3

Figure 18

COMPLETING THE QUILT

Step 1. Join three Small Ohio Star Variation blocks with two Large Ohio Star Variation blocks to make an X row referring to Figure 18; press seams toward the Large Ohio Star Variation blocks. Repeat to make three X rows.

Step 2. Join three Large Ohio Star Variation blocks with two Small Ohio Star Variation blocks to make a Y row, again referring to Figure 18; press seams toward the Large Ohio Star Variation blocks. Repeat to make three Y rows.

Step 3. Join the X and Y rows referring to the Placement Diagram to complete the pieced center; press seams toward the X rows.

Step 4. Sew O strips to opposite long sides and P strips to the top and bottom of the pieced center; press seams toward O and P strips.

Step 5. Sew R strips to opposite long sides of the pieced center; press seams toward R strips.

Step 6. Sew Q to each end of each S strip; press seams toward S strips.

Step 7. Sew an S-Q strip to the top and bottom of the pieced center; press seams toward S-Q strips.

Step 8. Sew a U strip to opposite long sides of the pieced center; press seams toward U strips.

Step 9. Sew T to each end of each V strip; press seams toward V. Sew the V-T strips to the top and bottom of the pieced center; press seams toward the V-T strips.

Step 10. Sew W strips to opposite long sides and X strips to the top and bottom of the pieced center to complete the top; press seams toward W and X strips.

Step 11. Complete the quilt using the previously cut binding strips and referring to Completing Your Quilt on page 170. ●

Stars Above
Placement Diagram
88" x 100"

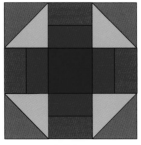
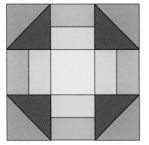

Dark Wrench
7½" x 7½" Block
Make 48

Light Wrench
7½" x 7½" Block
Make 35

Twisted Wrenches

The traditional Monkey Wrench quilt block is simple to piece with squares and triangles. Add some rectangles to replace the side squares and join the blocks on point to make another simple, but twisted version of this block.

PROJECT SPECIFICATIONS
Skill Level: Intermediate
Quilt Size: 79¾" x 101"
Block Size: 7½" x 7½"
Number of Blocks: 83

MATERIALS
- ⅝ yard pale peach tonal
- ⅞ yard each red, dark red, peach, salmon, light green and dark green tonals
- 1 yard light olive tonal
- 1⅛ yards darkest red tonal
- 3¼ yards dark olive tonal
- Backing 86" x 107"
- Batting 86" x 107"
- Neutral color all-purpose thread
- Quilting thread
- Basic sewing tools and supplies

CUTTING
Step 1. Cut four 3" by fabric width strips darkest red tonal; subcut strips into (48) 3" A squares.
Step 2. Cut eight 2½" by fabric width strips darkest red tonal. Join strips on short ends to make one long strip; press seams open. Subcut strip into two 85½" O strips and two 68¼" P strips.
Step 3. Cut (14) 1¾" by fabric width strips each dark red (B), red (C), peach (G) and salmon (H) tonals.
Step 4. Cut eight 3⅜" by fabric width strips each

light green (D) and dark green (E) tonals; sub-cut strips into (96) 3⅜" squares each. Cut each square on one diagonal to make 192 each D and E triangles.

Step 5. Cut three 3" by fabric width strips pale peach tonal; subcut strips into (35) 3" F squares.

Step 6. Cut one 4¾" by fabric width strip pale peach tonal; subcut strip into six 4¾" squares. Cut each square on both diagonals to make 24 K triangles.

Step 7. Cut two 2⅝" x 2⅝" squares pale peach tonal; cut each square in half on one diagonal to make four N triangles.

Step 8. Cut seven 3⅜" by fabric width strips each dark olive (I) and light olive (J) tonals; subcut strips into (82) 3⅜" squares each fabric. Cut each square in half on one diagonal to make 164 each I and J triangles.

Step 9. Cut two 2⅝" by fabric width strips each dark olive (L) and light olive (M) tonals; subcut strips into (28) 2⅝" squares each fabric. Cut each square in half on one diagonal to make 56 each L and M triangles.

Step 10. Cut nine 6½" by fabric width strips dark olive tonal. Join strips on short ends to make one long strip; press seams open. Subcut strip into two 89½" Q strips and two 80¼" R strips.

Step 11. Cut (10) 2¼" by fabric width strips dark olive tonal for binding.

PIECING THE DARK WRENCH BLOCKS

Step 1. Sew a B strip to a C strip with right sides together along the length; press seam toward B. Repeat to make 14 strip sets; subcut strip sets into (192) 3" B-C units as shown in Figure 1.

Figure 1   **Figure 2**

Step 2. Sew D to E to make a D-E unit as shown in Figure 2; repeat to make 96 D-E units. Press seams toward E.

Step 3. To complete one block, sew a B-C unit to opposite sides of A to make the center row as shown in Figure 3; press seams toward B-C units.

Figure 3

Step 4. Sew a D-E unit to opposite sides of a B-C unit to make a top row, again referring to Figure 3; press seams toward the B-C unit. Repeat to make the bottom row.

Step 5. Sew the center row between the top and bottom rows to complete one Dark Wrench block; press seams toward the center row. Repeat to make 48 blocks.

PIECING THE LIGHT WRENCH BLOCKS

Step 1. Sew a G strip to an H strip with right sides together along the length; press seam toward H. Repeat to make 14 strip sets; subcut strip sets into (192) 3" G-H units as shown in Figure 4.

Figure 4

Step 2. Sew I to J to make an I-J unit as shown in Figure 5; press seams toward I. Repeat to make 164 I-J units.

Figure 5

Step 3. To complete one Light Wrench block, sew a G-H unit to opposite sides of F to make the center row as shown in Figure 6; press seams toward F.

Figure 6

Step 4. Sew an I-J unit to opposite sides of a G-H unit to make the top row, again referring to Figure 6; press seams toward the G-H units. Repeat to make the bottom row.

Step 5. Sew the center row between the top and bottom rows to complete one block; press seams away from the center row. Repeat to make 35 blocks.

COMPLETING THE SIDE UNITS

Step 1. Sew L to M as shown in Figure 7; press seam toward L. Repeat to make 28 L-M units and 28 reversed L-M units.

Figure 7

Step 2. To piece one side unit, sew an I-J unit to one side of a G-H unit as shown in Figure 8; press seams toward the G-H unit.

Figure 8

Step 3. Sew an L-M unit to the G-H-I-J unit to make an M unit as shown in Figure 9; press seams toward L-M.

Figure 9

Step 4. Sew K and a reversed L-M unit to adjacent sides of a G-H unit to make a K unit as shown in Figure 10; press seams toward K and L-M.

Figure 10

Step 5. Join the K unit with the M unit to complete one side unit as shown in Figure 11;

press seam toward the K unit. Repeat to make 24 side units.

Figure 11

COMPLETING THE CORNER UNITS

Step 1. To piece one corner unit, sew an L-M unit and a reversed L-M unit to opposite sides of a G-H unit as shown in Figure 12; press seams toward L-M units.

Figure 12

Step 2. Add N to the G side of the pieced unit to complete one corner unit, again referring to Figure 12; press seam toward N. Repeat to make four corner units.

COMPLETING THE QUILT

Step 1. Arrange the blocks with the side and corner units in diagonal rows as shown in Figure 13; join to make rows. Press seams in adjoining rows in opposite directions.

Figure 13

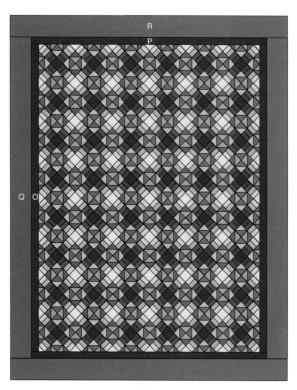

Twisted Wrenches
Placement Diagram
79³/4" x 101"

Step 2. Join the rows to complete the pieced top referring to the Placement Diagram for positioning; press seams in one direction.

Step 3. Sew O strips to opposite sides and P strips to the top and bottom of the pieced center; press seams toward the O and P strips.

Step 4. Sew Q strips to opposite sides and R strips to the top and bottom of the pieced center to complete the top; press seams toward the Q and R strips.

Step 5. Complete the quilt using the previously cut binding strips and referring to Completing Your Quilt on page 170. ●

design by **JULIE WEAVER**

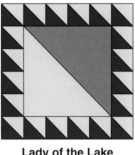

Lady of the Lake
12" x 12" Block

Lake in the Woods

Placement and coloration of the traditional Lady of the Lake

block creates a contemporary masculine quilt. Twist and turn the

blocks, sew them together with a simple sashing and watch the

paths appear. An added bonus is the interesting patterns created

by the block's half-square triangles and the sashing.

PROJECT SPECIFICATIONS
Skill Level: Beginner
Quilt Size: 88" x 101½"
Block Size: 12" x 12"
Number of Blocks: 30

MATERIALS
- ½ yard dark blue tonal
- 1¼ yards total brown prints
- 1½ yards brown stripe
- 1⅝ yards brown/black print
- 2 yards total navy tonals
- 2 yards brown plaid
- 3 yards cream mottled
- Backing 94" x 107"
- Batting 94" x 107"
- Neutral color all-purpose thread
- Quilting thread
- Basic sewing tools and supplies

CUTTING
Step 1. Cut four 8⅞" by fabric width strips cream
mottled; subcut strips into (15) 8⅞" A squares.
Mark a diagonal line from corner to corner on the
wrong side of each square.
Step 2. Cut (22) 2⅞" by fabric width strips cream

mottled; subcut strips into (300) 2⅞" C squares. Mark a diagonal line from corner to corner on the wrong side of each square.

Step 3. Cut a total of (15) 8⅞" x 8⅞" B squares from brown prints. **Note:** *The sample quilt used 15 different brown prints.*

Step 4. Cut a total of (300) 2⅞" x 2⅞" squares from navy tonals. **Note:** *The sample quilt used 10 squares from 30 different navy tonals.*

Step 5. Cut four 12½" by fabric width strips brown stripe; subcut strips into (71) 2" E strips.

Step 6. Cut two 2" by fabric width strips dark blue tonal; subcut strips into (42) 2" F squares.

Step 7. Cut eight 1½" x 1½" I squares and four 8" x 8" L squares dark blue tonal.

Step 8. Cut (17) 1½" by fabric width strips brown/black print. Join strips on short ends to make one long strip; press seams open. Subcut strip into two strips each 83" G, 69½" H, 100" M and 86½" N.

Step 9. Cut eight 8" by fabric width strips brown plaid. Join strips on short ends to make one long strip; press seams open. Subcut strip into two 85" J strips and two 71½" K strips.

Step 10. Cut (10) 2¼" by fabric width strips brown/black print for binding.

PIECING THE BLOCKS

Step 1. Place an A square right sides together with a B square; stitch ¼" on each side of the marked line as shown in Figure 1. Cut apart on the marked line to make two A-B units as shown in Figure 2; press seams toward B. Repeat to make 30 A-B units.

Figure 1   **Figure 2**

Step 2. To complete one Lady of the Lake block, select 10 same-fabric D squares. Place a C square right sides together with a D square; stitch ¼" on each side of the marked line as in Step 1.

Step 3. Cut apart on the marked line to make two C-D units as shown in Figure 3; press seams toward D. Repeat with the remaining C and D squares to make 20 C-D units.

Figure 3

Step 4. Join four C-D units to make a side row as shown in Figure 4; repeat to make two side rows. Press seams in one direction.

Figure 4

Step 5. Sew the side rows to opposite sides of one A-B unit as shown in Figure 5; press seams toward the A-B unit.

Figure 5

Step 6. Join six C-D units to make a top row as shown in Figure 6; repeat to make the bottom row. Press seams in one direction.

Figure 6

Step 7. Sew the top and bottom rows to the remaining sides of the A-B unit referring to the block drawing to complete one block; press seams toward the A-B unit. Repeat to make 30 blocks.

COMPLETING THE QUILT

Step 1. Join five Lady of the Lake blocks with six E strips to make a block row referring to Figure 7; press seams toward E. Repeat to make six block rows referring to the Placement Diagram for placement of blocks in each row.

Figure 7

Step 2. Join five E strips with six F squares to make a sashing row; press seams toward E. Repeat to make seven sashing rows.

Step 3. Join the block rows with the sashing rows to complete the pieced center; press seams toward sashing rows.

Step 4. Sew G strips to opposite long sides; press seams toward G strips.

Step 5. Sew an I square to each end of each H strip; press seams toward H strips. Sew the H-I strips to the top and bottom of the pieced center; press seams toward H-I strips.

Step 6. Sew J strips to opposite long sides of the pieced center; press seams toward J strips.

Step 7. Sew an L square to each end of each K strip; press seams toward K strips. Sew the K-L strips to the top and bottom of the pieced center; press seams toward K-L strips.

Step 8. Sew M strips to opposite long sides of the pieced center; press seams toward M strips.

Step 9. Sew an I square to each end of each N strip; press seams toward N strips. Sew the I-N strips to the top and bottom of the pieced center to complete the top; press seams toward I-N strips.

Step 10. Complete the quilt using the previously cut binding strips and referring to Completing Your Quilt on page 170. ●

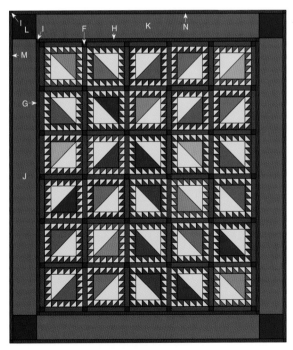

Lake in the Woods
Placement Diagram
88" x 101½"

X Marks the Spot
12" x 12" Block

X Marks the Spot

The traditional Square-in-a-Square block has an added piece in the corner triangles that forms an X design when sashing rows with squares are used to join the blocks. The pattern is deceiving. The X design is not the block.

PROJECT SPECIFICATIONS
Skill Level: Beginner
Quilt Size: 76" x 90"
Block Size: 12" x 12"
Number of Blocks: 20

MATERIALS
- ⅔ yard blue stripe
- 1½ yards medium green tonal
- 1½ yards dark green tonal
- 2 yards cream tonal
- 2½ yards blue paisley
- Backing 82" x 96"
- Batting 82" x 96"
- Neutral color all-purpose thread
- Quilting thread
- Basic sewing tools and supplies

CUTTING
Step 1. Cut four 6⅞" by fabric width strips each blue paisley (A) and medium green tonal (B); subcut strips into (20) 6⅞" squares each fabric. Cut each square in half on one diagonal to make 40 each A and B triangles.

Step 2. Cut seven 2½" by fabric width strips medium green tonal. Join strips on short ends to make one long strip; press seams open. Subcut strip into two 74½" I strips and two 64½" J strips.

Step 3. Cut eight 6½" by fabric width strips blue paisley. Join strips on short ends to make one long

strip; press seams open. Subcut strip into two 78½" K strips and two 76½" L strips.

Step 4. Cut two 2½" by fabric width strips blue paisley; subcut strips into (30) 2½" E squares.

Step 5. Cut five 5" by fabric width strips cream tonal; subcut strips into (80) 2⅝" C rectangles.

Step 6. Cut three 12½" by fabric width strips cream tonal; subcut strips into (48) 2½" F strips. Cut one additional 2½" x 12½" F strip.

Step 7. Cut six 5¾" by fabric width strips dark green tonal; subcut strips into (40) 5¾" squares. Cut each square on both diagonals to make 160 D triangles.

Step 8. Cut seven 1½" by fabric width strips dark green tonal. Join strips on short ends to make one long strip; press seams open. Subcut strip into two 72½" G strips and two 60½" H strips.

Step 9. Cut nine 2¼" by fabric width strips blue stripe for binding.

PIECING THE BLOCKS

Step 1. To piece one block, sew A to B as shown in Figure 1; repeat to make two A-B units. Press seams toward B.

Figure 1

Step 2. Join the two A-B units to complete the block center as shown in Figure 2; carefully press seams in one direction to avoid stretching the bias edges of the unit.

Figure 2

Step 3. Sew a D triangle to opposite long sides of C to make a C-D unit as shown in Figure 3; press seams toward D. Repeat to make four C-D units.

Figure 3

Step 4. Using a rotary ruler and cutter, trim C even with the angle of the D pieces in each C-D unit as shown in Figure 4.

Figure 4

Step 5. Sew a C-D unit to each side of the A-B unit to complete one block referring to Figure 5; press seams toward A or B. Repeat to make 20 blocks.

Figure 5

COMPLETING THE QUILT

Step 1. Join four blocks with five F strips to complete a block row as shown in Figure 6; press seams toward F. Repeat to make five rows.

Figure 6

Step 2. Join five E squares with four F strips to make a sashing row as shown in Figure 7; press seams toward F. Repeat to make six sashing rows.

Figure 7

Step 3. Join the block rows with the sashing rows referring to the Placement Diagram for positioning; press seams toward sashing rows.

Step 4. Sew G strips to opposite sides and H strips to the top and bottom of the pieced center; press seams toward G and H strips.

Step 5. Sew I strips to opposite sides and J strips to the top and bottom of the pieced center; press seams toward I and J strips.

Step 6. Sew K strips to opposite sides and L strips to the top and bottom of the pieced center to complete the top; press seams toward K and L strips.

Step 7. Complete the quilt using the previously cut binding strips and referring to Completing Your Quilt on page 170. ●

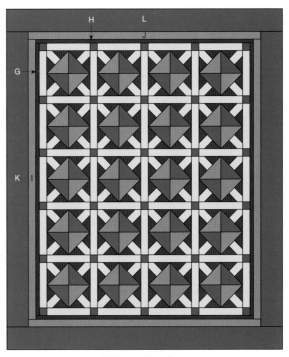

X Marks the Spot
Placement Diagram
76" x 90"

design by **LINDA MILLER**

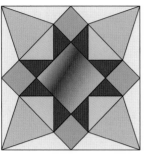

Large Dogtooth Violet
13½" x 13½" Block
Make 1

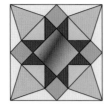

Small Dogtooth Violet
9" x 9" Block
Make 16

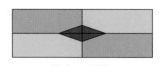

Twisted Tie
4½" x 13½" Block
Make 16

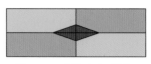

Reversed Twisted Tie
4½" x 13½" Block
Make 12

Bow Tie
4½" x 4½" Block
Make 12

Twisted Ties

The blocks in this quilt are sewn together in a twisting and turning path seemingly without rhyme or reason. The result is a stunning quilt.

PROJECT SPECIFICATIONS

Skill Level: Advanced
Quilt Size: 71½" x 71½"
Block Size: 13½" x 13½", 9" x 9", 4½" x 13½" and 4½" x 4½"
Number of Blocks: 1, 16, 28 and 12

MATERIALS

All fabrics are batiks.
- ¾ yard tan/gray mottled
- 1⅛ yards tan mottled
- 1¼ yards green mottled
- 1⅜ yards rose mottled
- 1⅝ yards gold mottled
- 2 yards multicolor mottled
- Backing 78" x 78"
- Batting 78" x 78"
- Neutral color all-purpose thread
- Quilting thread
- Basic sewing tools and supplies

CUTTING

Step 1. Prepare templates for pieces A–N using patterns given; cut as directed on each piece.
Step 2. Cut two 2¾" by fabric width strips each gold (O) and rose (P) mottleds; subcut strips into (24) 2¾" each O and P squares.
Step 3. Cut two 1¼" by fabric width strips green mottled; subcut strips into (48) 1¼" Q squares. Draw a diagonal line from corner to corner on the wrong side of each Q square.
Step 4. Cut six 2" by fabric width strips green mottled. Join strips on short ends to make one long strip; press seams open. Subcut strips into two 59" R strips and two 62" S strips.
Step 5. Cut seven 5½" by fabric width strips multicolor mottled. Join strips on short ends to make one long strip; press seams open. Subcut strips into two 62" T strips and two 72" U strips.
Step 6. Cut eight 2¼" by fabric width strips multicolor mottled for binding.

PIECING THE LARGE DOGTOOTH VIOLET BLOCK

Step 1. To piece the Large Dogtooth Violet block, sew C to two adjacent short sides of B as shown in Figure 1; press seams toward C. Repeat to make four B-C units.

Figure 1 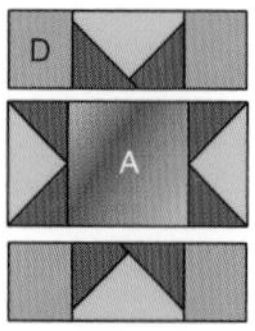   Figure 2

Step 2. Sew a B-C unit to opposite sides of A as shown in Figure 2; press seams toward A.

Step 3. Sew D to each end of each remaining B-C unit; press seams toward D. Sew these B-C-D units to the remaining sides of A to complete the center unit, again referring to Figure 2.

Step 4. Sew F and FR to E to make a corner unit as shown in Figure 3; press seams toward F and FR.

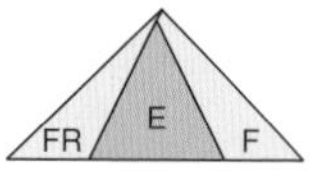

Figure 3

Step 5. Sew a corner unit to each side of the center unit to complete the block referring to the block drawing; press seams toward the corner units.

PIECING THE SMALL DOGTOOTH VIOLET BLOCKS

Step 1. Piece 16 Small Dogtooth Violet blocks as for Large Dogtooth blocks referring to Figure 4 to piece the center unit with pieces G, H, I and J and to Figure 5 to piece the corner units with pieces K, L and LR.

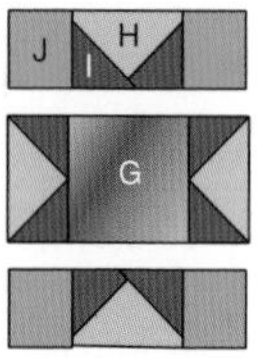

Figure 4 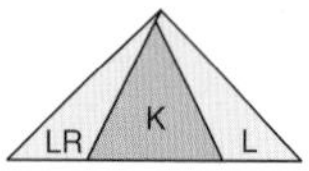   Figure 5

PIECING THE TWISTED TIE BLOCKS

Step 1. Sew N to M and NR to MR as shown in Figure 6; press seams toward M and MR. Repeat to make two each M-N and MR-NR units.

Figure 6

Step 2. Sew an MR-NR unit to an M-N unit as shown in Figure 7; press seams toward M-N units. Repeat to complete two units.

Figure 7

Step 3. Join the two pieced units on the N/NR ends to complete one Twisted Tie block referring to the block drawing; press seam in one direction. Repeat to make 16 Twisted Tie blocks and 12 Reversed Twisted Tie blocks.

PIECING THE BOW TIE BLOCKS

Step 1. Place a Q square right sides together on one corner of O referring to Figure 8; stitch on the marked line. Trim seam to ¼" and press Q to the right side; repeat on all O and P squares.

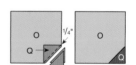

Figure 8

Step 2. Sew an O-Q unit to a P-Q unit as shown in Figure 9; press seams toward the P-Q unit. Repeat with all units.

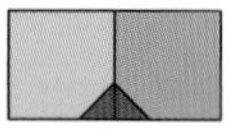

Figure 9

Step 3. To complete one block, join two O-Q-P-Q units referring to the block drawing; press seams in one direction. Repeat to make 12 blocks.

COMPLETING THE QUILT

Step 1. Join two Twisted Tie blocks as shown in Figure 10; press seam in one direction. Repeat for four joined-block units.

Figure 10

Step 2. Sew a joined-block unit to opposite sides of the Large Dogtooth Violet block to make the center row as shown in Figure 11; press seams toward the joined-block units.

Figure 11

Step 3. Sew a Small Dogtooth Violet block to each end of each remaining joined-block unit to make the top and bottom rows as shown in Figure 12; press seams toward the joined-block units.

Figure 12

Step 4. Sew the top and bottom rows to the center row to complete the quilt center as shown in Figure 13; press seams away from the center row.

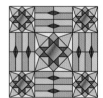

Figure 13

Step 5. Join one Small Dogtooth Violet block with one each Bow Tie and Twisted Tie block to make a one-block unit referring to Figure 14; repeat to make a reversed one-block unit using a Reversed Twisted Tie block, again referring to

Figure 14. Repeat to make four one-block units and four reversed one-block units; press seams away from the Small Dogtooth Violet blocks.

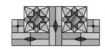

Figure 14   **Figure 15**

Step 6. Join a one-block unit and a reversed one-block unit with a Reversed Twisted Tie block to make a side row as shown in Figure 15; press seams away from the one-block units. Repeat to make two side rows.

Step 7. Sew a side row to opposite sides of the pieced center as shown in Figure 16; press seams away from the pieced center.

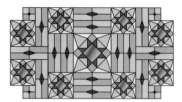

Figure 16

Step 8. Add a Small Dogtooth Violet block and a Twisted Tie block to the remaining one-block units to complete a two-block unit, setting in blocks as needed referring to Figure 17; press seams away from the Small Dogtooth Violet blocks. Repeat to make two reversed two-block units using Reversed Twisted Tie blocks, again referring to Figure 17.

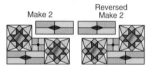

Figure 17

Step 9. Join a two-block unit and a reversed two-block unit with a Reversed Twisted Tie block to make a side unit as shown in Figure 18; press seams away from the two-block units. Repeat to make two side units.

Figure 18

Step 10. Sew the side units to opposite sides of the pieced center; press seams away from the pieced center.

Step 11. Sew a Bow Tie block to a Twisted Tie block to make a corner unit as shown in Figure 19; press seam toward the Bow Tie block. Repeat to make two corner units.

Figure 19

Step 12. Repeat Step 11 with Bow Tie blocks and Reversed Twisted Tie blocks to make two reversed corner units, again referring to Figure 19.

Step 13. Set the corner units in at the corners referring to the Placement Diagram for positioning to complete the pieced center; press seams toward corner units.

Step 14. Sew an R strip to opposite sides and S strips to the top and bottom of the pieced center; press seams toward R and S strips.

Step 15. Sew a T strip to opposite sides and U strips to the top and bottom of the pieced center; press seams toward T and U strips.

Step 16. Complete the quilt using the previously cut binding strips and referring to Completing Your Quilt on page 170. ●

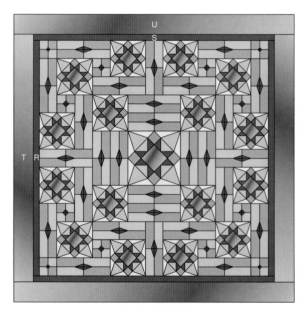

Twisted Ties
Placement Diagram
71½" x 71½"

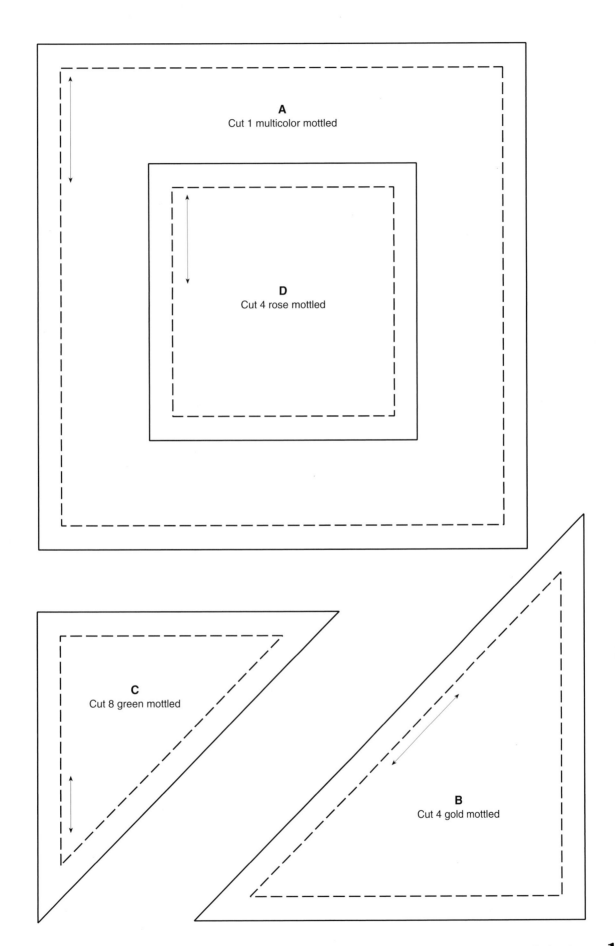

A
Cut 1 multicolor mottled

D
Cut 4 rose mottled

C
Cut 8 green mottled

B
Cut 4 gold mottled

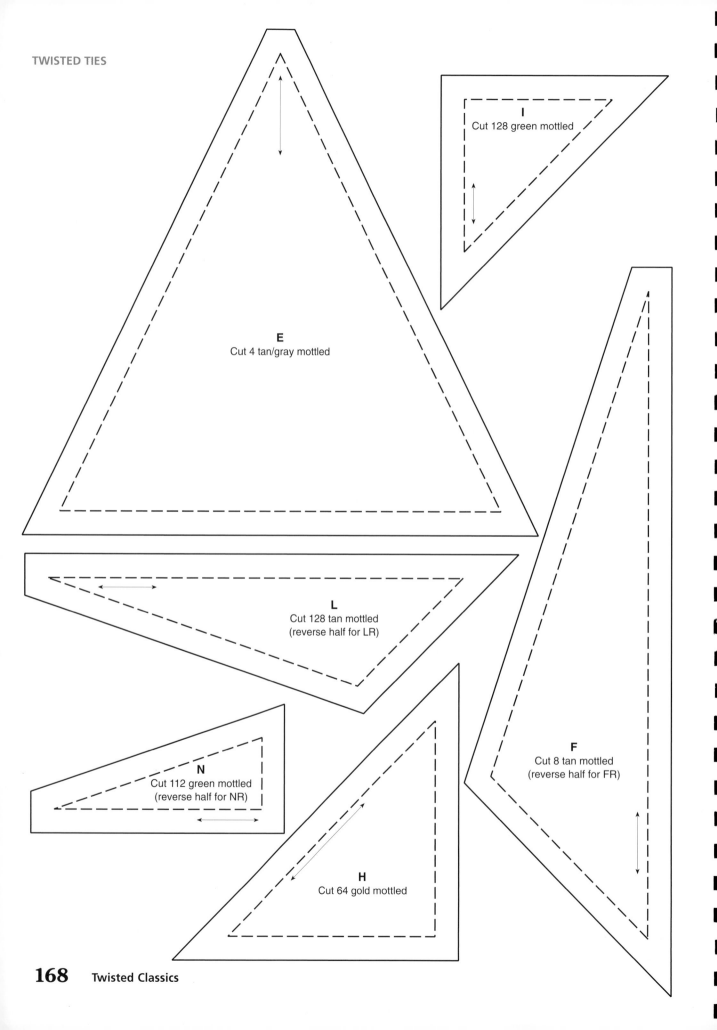

I
Cut 128 green mottled

E
Cut 4 tan/gray mottled

L
Cut 128 tan mottled
(reverse half for LR)

N
Cut 112 green mottled
(reverse half for NR)

F
Cut 8 tan mottled
(reverse half for FR)

H
Cut 64 gold mottled

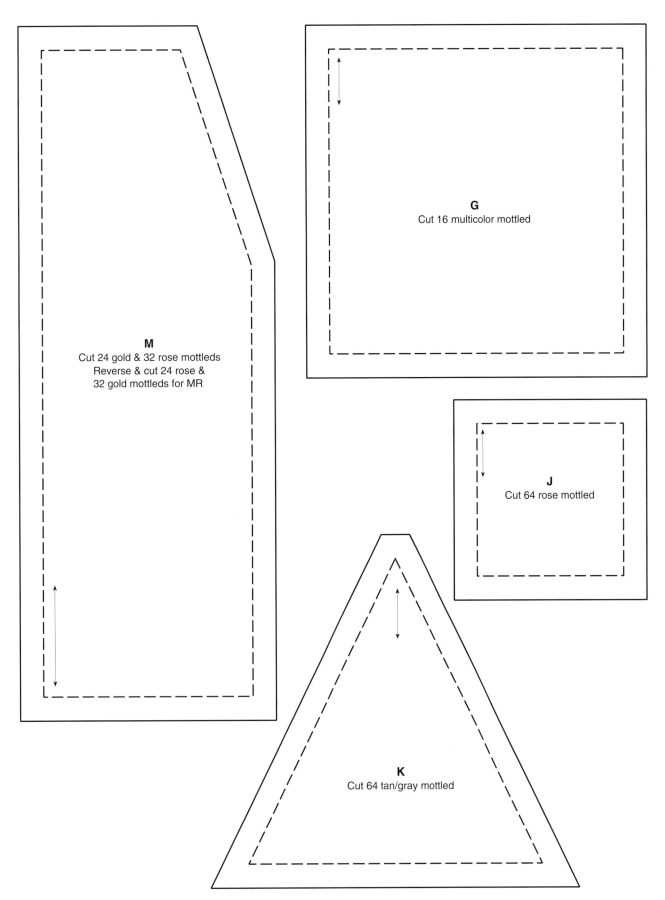

M
Cut 24 gold & 32 rose mottleds
Reverse & cut 24 rose &
32 gold mottleds for MR

G
Cut 16 multicolor mottled

J
Cut 64 rose mottled

K
Cut 64 tan/gray mottled

Completing Your Quilt

Finishing the Top

Settings. Most quilts are made by sewing individual blocks together in rows that, when joined, create a design. There are several other methods used to join blocks. Sometimes the setting choice is determined by the block's design. For example, a House block should be placed upright on a quilt, not sideways or upside down.

Plain blocks can be alternated with pieced or appliquéd blocks in a straight set. Making a quilt using plain blocks saves time; half the number of pieced or appliquéd blocks are needed to make the same-size quilt as shown in Figure 1.

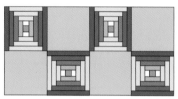

Figure 1

Adding Borders. Borders are an integral part of the quilt and should complement the colors and designs used in the quilt center. Borders frame a quilt just like a mat and frame do a picture.

If fabric strips are added for borders, they may be mitered or butted at the corners as shown in Figures 2 and 3. To determine the size for butted border strips, measure across the center of the completed quilt top from one side raw edge to the other side raw edge. This measurement will include a ¼" seam allowance.

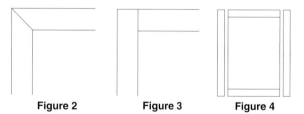

| **Figure 2** | **Figure 3** | **Figure 4** |

Cut two border strips that length by the chosen width of the border. Sew these strips to the top and bottom of the pieced center referring to Figure 4. Press the seam allowance toward the border strips.

Measure across the completed quilt top at the center,

from top raw edge to bottom raw edge, including the two border strips already added. Cut two border strips that length by the chosen width of the border. Sew a strip to each of the two remaining sides as shown in Figure 4. Press the seams toward the border strips.

To make mitered corners, measure the quilt as before. To this add twice the width of the border and ½" for seam allowances to determine the length of the strips. Repeat for opposite sides. Sew on each strip, stopping stitching ¼" from corner, leaving the remainder of the strip dangling.

Press corners at a 45-degree angle to form a crease. Stitch from the inside quilt corner to the outside on the creased line. Trim excess away after stitching and press mitered seams open (Figures 5–7).

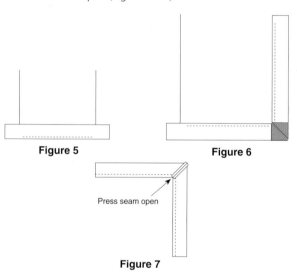

| **Figure 5** | **Figure 6** |

Press seam open

Figure 7

Carefully press the entire piece, including the pieced center. Avoid pulling and stretching while pressing, which would distort shapes.

Getting Ready to Quilt

Choosing a Quilting Design.

If you choose to hand- or machine-quilt your finished top, you will need to select a design for quilting.

There are several types of quilting designs, some of which may not have to be marked. The easiest of the unmarked designs is in-the-ditch quilting. Here the quilting stitches are placed in the valley created by the seams joining two pieces together or next to the edge of an appliqué design. There is no need to mark a top for in-the-ditch quilting. Machine quilters choose this option because the stitches are not as obvious on the finished quilt (Figure 8).

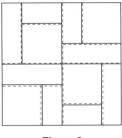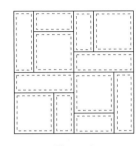

| Figure 8 | Figure 9 |

Outline-quilting ¼" or more away from seams or appliqué shapes is another no-mark alternative (Figure 9) that prevents having to sew through the layers made by seams, thus making stitching easier.

If you are not comfortable eyeballing the ¼" (or other distance), masking tape is available in different widths and is helpful to place on straight-edge designs to mark the quilting line. If using masking tape, place the tape right up against the seam and quilt close to the other edge.

Meander or free-motion quilting by machine fills in open spaces and doesn't require marking. It is fun and easy to stitch as shown in Figure 10.

Figure 10

Marking the Top for Quilting. If you choose a

fancy or allover design for quilting, you will need to transfer the design to your quilt top before layering with the backing and batting. You may use a sharp medium-lead or silver pencil on light background fabrics. Test the pencil marks to guarantee that they will wash out of your quilt top when quilting is complete; or be sure your quilting stitches cover the pencil marks. Mechanical pencils with very fine points may be used successfully to mark quilts.

Manufactured quilt-design templates are available in many designs and sizes and are cut out of a durable plastic template material that is easy to use.

To make a permanent quilt-design template, choose a template material on which to transfer the design. See-through plastic is the best because it will let you place the design while allowing you to see where it is in relation to your quilt design without moving it. Place the design on the quilt top where you want it and trace around it with your marking tool. Pick up the quilting template and place again; repeat marking.

No matter what marking method you use, remember—the marked lines should never show on the finished quilt. When the top is marked, it is ready for layering.

Preparing the Quilt Backing. The quilt backing is a very important feature of your quilt. The materials listed for each quilt in this book include the size requirements for the backing, not the yardage needed. Exceptions to this are when the backing fabric is also used on the quilt top and yardage is given for that fabric.

A backing is generally cut at least 6" larger than the quilt top or 2" larger on all sides. For a 64" x 78" finished quilt, the backing would need to be at least 70" x 84".

To avoid having the seam across the center of the quilt backing, cut or tear one of the right-length pieces in half, and sew half to each side of the second piece as shown in Figure 11.

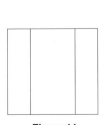

| Figure 11 | Figure 12 |

Quilts that need a backing more than 88" wide may be pieced in horizontal pieces as shown in Figure 12.

Layering the Quilt Sandwich. Layering the quilt top with the batting and backing is time-consuming. Open the batting several days before you need it and place over a bed or flat on the floor to help flatten the creases caused from its being folded up in the bag for so long.

Iron the backing piece, folding in half both vertically and horizontally and pressing to mark centers.

If you will not be quilting on a frame, place the backing right side down on a clean floor or table. Start in the center and push any wrinkles or bunches flat. Use masking tape to tape the edges to the floor or large clips to hold the backing to the edges of the table. The backing should be taut.

Place the batting on top of the backing, matching centers using fold lines as guides; flatten out any wrinkles. Trim the batting to the same size as the backing. Fold the quilt top in half lengthwise and place on top of the batting, wrong side against the batting, matching centers. Unfold quilt and, working from the center to the outside edges, smooth out any wrinkles or lumps.

To hold the quilt layers together for quilting, baste by hand or use safety pins. If basting by hand, thread a long thin needle with a long piece of unknotted white or off-white thread. Starting in the center and leaving a long tail, make 4"–6" stitches toward the outside edge of the quilt top, smoothing as you baste. Start at the center again and work toward the outside as shown in Figure 13.

Figure 13

If quilting by machine, you may prefer to use safety pins for holding your fabric sandwich together. Start in the center of the quilt and pin to the outside, leaving pins open until all are placed. When you are satisfied that all layers are smooth, close the pins.

Quilting

Hand Quilting. Hand quilting is the process of placing stitches through the quilt top, batting and backing to hold them together. While it is a functional process, it also adds beauty and loft to the finished quilt.

To begin, thread a sharp between needle with an 18" piece of quilting thread. Tie a small knot in the end of the thread. Position the needle about ½"–1" away from the starting point on quilt top. Sink the needle through the top into the batting layer but not through the backing. Pull the needle up at the starting point of the quilting design. Pull the needle and thread until the knot sinks through the top into the batting (Figure 14).

Figure 14   **Figure 15**

Some stitchers like to take a backstitch here at the beginning while others prefer to begin the first stitch here. Take small, even running stitches along the marked quilting line (Figure 15). Keep one hand positioned underneath to feel the needle go all the way through to the backing.

When you have nearly run out of thread, wind the thread around the needle several times to make a small knot and pull it close to the fabric. Insert the needle into the fabric on the quilting line and come out with the needle ½"–1" away, pulling the knot into the fabric layers the same as when you started. Pull and cut thread close to fabric. The end should disappear inside after cutting. Some quilters prefer to take a backstitch with a loop through it for a knot to end.

Machine Quilting. Successful machine quilting requires practice and a good relationship with your sewing machine.

Prepare the quilt for machine quilting in the same way as for hand quilting. Use safety pins to hold the layers together instead of basting with thread.

Presser-foot quilting is best used for straight-line quilting because the presser bar lever does not need to be continually lifted.

Set the machine on a longer stitch length (3.0 or 8–10 stitches to the inch). Too tight a stitch causes puckering and fabric tucks, either on the quilt top or backing. An even-feed or walking foot helps to eliminate the tucks and puckering by feeding the upper and lower layers through the machine evenly. Before you begin, loosen the amount of pressure on the presser foot.

Special machine-quilting needles work best to penetrate the three layers in your quilt.

Finishing the Edges

After your quilt is tied or quilted, the edges need to be finished. Decide how you want the edges of your quilt finished before layering the backing and batting with the quilt top.

Without Binding—Self-Finish. There is one way to eliminate adding an edge finish. This is done before quilting. Place the batting on a flat surface. Place the pieced top right side up on the batting. Place the backing right sides together with the pieced top. Pin and/or baste the layers together to hold flat referring to Layering the Quilt Sandwich.

Begin stitching in the center of one side using a ¼" seam allowance, reversing at the beginning and end of the seam. Continue stitching all around and back to the beginning side. Leave a 12" or larger opening. Clip corners to reduce excess. Turn right side out through the opening. Slipstitch the opening closed by hand. The quilt may now be quilted by hand or machine.

The disadvantage to this method is that once the edges are sewn in, any creases or wrinkles that might form during the quilting process cannot be flattened out. Tying is the preferred method for finishing a quilt constructed using this method.

Bringing the backing fabric to the front is another way to finish the quilt's edge without binding. To accomplish this, complete the quilt as for hand or machine quilting. Trim the batting only even with the front. Trim the backing 1" larger than the completed top all around.

Turn the backing edge in ½" and then turn over to the front along edge of batting. The folded edge may be machine-stitched close to the edge through all layers or blind-stitched in place to finish.

The front may be turned to the back. If using this method, a wider front border is needed. The backing and batting are trimmed 1" smaller than the top, and the top edge is turned under ½" and then turned to the back and stitched in place.

Binding. The technique of adding extra fabric at the edges of the quilt is called binding. The binding encloses the edges and adds an extra layer of fabric for durability.

To prepare the quilt for the addition of the binding, trim the batting and backing layers flush with the top of the quilt using a rotary cutter and ruler or shears. Using a walking-foot attachment (sometimes called an even-feed foot attachment), machine-baste the three layers together all around approximately ⅛" from the cut edge.

Bias binding may be purchased in packages and in many colors. The advantage to self-made binding is that you can use fabrics from your quilt to coordinate colors. Double-fold, straight-grain binding and double-fold, bias-grain binding are two of the most commonly used types of binding.

Double-fold, straight-grain binding is used on smaller projects with right-angle corners. Double-fold, bias-grain binding is best suited for bed-size quilts or quilts with rounded corners.

To make double-fold, straight-grain binding, cut 2¼"-wide strips of fabric across the width or down the length of the fabric totaling the perimeter of the quilt plus 10". The strips are joined as shown in Figure 16 and pressed in half wrong sides together along the length using an iron on a cotton setting with no steam.

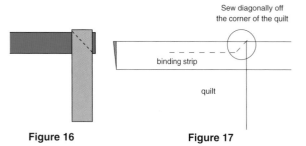

Figure 16   **Figure 17**

Lining up the raw edges, place the binding on the top of the quilt and begin sewing (again using the walking foot) approximately 6" from the beginning of the binding strip. Stop sewing ¼" from the first corner, leave the needle in the quilt, turn and sew diagonally to the corner as shown in Figure 17.

Fold the binding at a 45-degree angle up and away from the quilt as shown in Figure 18 and back down flush with the raw edges. Starting at the top raw edge of the quilt, begin sewing the next side as shown in Figure 19. Repeat at the next three corners.

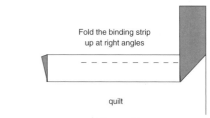

Figure 18

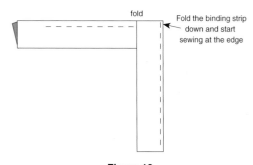

Figure 19

As you approach the beginning of the binding strip, stop stitching and overlap the binding ½" from the edge; trim. Join the two ends with a ¼" seam allowance and press the seam open. Reposition the joined binding along the edge of the quilt and resume stitching to the beginning.

To finish, bring the folded edge of the binding over the raw edges and blind-stitch the binding in place over the machine-stitching line on the back side. Hand-miter the corners on the back as shown in Figure 20.

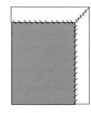

Figure 20

To make double-fold, bias-grain binding, cut 2¼"-wide bias strips from a large square of fabric. Join the strips as illustrated in Figure 16 and press the seams open. Fold the beginning end of the bias strip ¼" from the raw edge and press. Fold the joined strips in half along the long side, wrong sides together, and press with no steam (Figure 21).

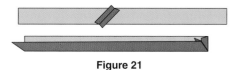

Figure 21

Follow the same procedures as previously described for preparing the quilt top and sewing the binding to the quilt top. Treat the corners just as you treated them with straight-grain binding.

Since you are using bias-grain binding, you do have the option to just eliminate the corners if this option doesn't interfere with the patchwork in the quilt. Round the corners off by placing one of your dinner plates at the corner and rotary-cutting the gentle curve (Figure 22).

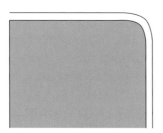

Figure 22

As you approach the beginning of the binding strip, stop stitching and lay the end across the beginning so it will slip inside the fold. Cut the end at a 45-degree angle so the raw edges are contained inside the beginning of the strip (Figure 23). Resume stitching to the beginning. Bring the fold to the back of the quilt and hand-stitch as previously described.

Figure 23

Overlapped corners are not quite as easy as rounded ones, but they are a bit easier than mitering. To make over-lapped corners, sew binding strips to opposite sides of the quilt top. Stitch edges down to finish. Trim ends even.

Sew a strip to each remaining side, leaving 1½"–2" excess at each end. Turn quilt over and fold binding down even with previous finished edge as shown in Figure 24.

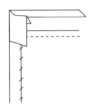

Figure 24

Fold binding in toward quilt and stitch down as before, enclosing the previous bound edge in the seam as shown in Figure 25. It may be necessary to trim the folded-down section to reduce bulk.

Figure 25

Instead of cutting individual bias strips and sewing them together, you may make continuous bias binding.

Cut a square 21" x 21" from chosen binding fabric. Cut the square once on the diagonal to make two triangles as shown in Figure 26. With right sides together, join the two triangles with a ¼" seam allowance as shown in Figure 27; press seam open to reduce bulk.

Figure 26   **Figure 27**

Mark lines every 2¼" on the wrong side of the fabric as shown in Figure 28. Bring the short ends together, right sides together, offsetting one line as shown in Figure 29; stitch to make a tube. This will seem awkward.

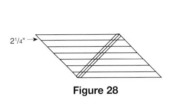

Figure 28

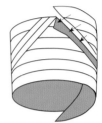

Figure 29

Begin cutting at point A as shown in Figure 30; continue cutting along marked line to make one continuous strip. Fold strip in half along length with wrong sides together; press. Sew to quilt edges as instructed previously for bias binding.

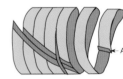

Figure 30

Final Touches

If your quilt will be hung on the wall, a hanging sleeve is required. Other options include purchased plastic rings or fabric tabs. The best choice is a fabric sleeve, which will evenly distribute the weight of the quilt across the top edge, rather than at selected spots where tabs or rings are stitched, keep the quilt hanging straight and not damage the batting.

When the quilt is finally complete, it should be signed and dated. Use a permanent pen on the back of the quilt. Other methods include cross-stitching your name and date on the front or back or making a permanent label which may be stitched to the back. ●

Special Thanks

We would like to thank the talented quilt designers whose work is featured in this collection.

Pat Campbell
Chained Nine-Patch, 11

Holly Daniels
Autumn Garden, 55
Morning Glorious, 6

Lucy A. Fazely & Michael L. Burns
Garden Affair, 102
Impulse, 110

Sandra L. Hatch
Amish Skies, 83
Rectangle Parade, 121
X Marks the Spot, 159

Connie Kauffman
Pathway to the Stars, 22
Piney Woods, 33

Linda Miller
Diamond Twist, 130
Different Twist, 16
Tumbling Twister, 115
Twisted Ties, 162

Sue Harvey & Sandy Boobar
Ladies of the Lake, 125
Midnight Paths, 90
Star to Star, 139

Jill Reber
Blue Ribbon Twist, 47

Judith Sandstrom
Black Tie, 94
Southwest Stars, 74

Marian Shenk
Disoriented Dancing Stars, 26
Drunkard's Path Tulip Garden, 40

Cate Tallman-Evans
Prairie Garden, 98
Twisted Wrenches, 149

Rhonda Taylor
Wind Dust Florets, 78

Julie Weaver
Autumn Air, 106
Autumn Song Table Runner, 64
Bountiful Harvest, 60
Garden of the Bear, 69
Holiday Splendor, 86
Lake in the Woods, 154
Stars Above, 144

Johanna Wilson
Changing Seasons, 50
Solitude Medallion, 135

Fabrics & Supplies

Page 16: Different Twist—Teahouse Garden fabric collection from RJR Fabrics. Machine-quilted by Lillian Lee.

Page 33: Piney Woods—Hobbs Fusible Batting and Sulky® cotton threads.

Page 47: Blue Ribbon Twist—Master Piece 45 Ruler and Static Stickers from Master Piece Products and Pfaff sewing machine.

Page 60: Bountiful Harvest—Warm & Natural cotton batting from The Warm Co.

Page 64: Autumn Song Table Runner—Warm & Natural cotton batting from The Warm Co.

Page 69: Garden of the Bear—Warm & Natural cotton batting from The Warm Co.

Page 74: Southwest Stars—Fiskars rotary cutting tools and DMC quilting thread and needles.

Page 78: Wind Dust Florets—Machine-quilted by Sandy Boobar.

Page 83: Amish Skies—Fabrics provided by Diamond Textiles, White Rose cotton batting from Mountain Mist and Star Machine Quilting thread from Coats. Machine-quilted by Dianne Hodgkins.

Page 86: Holiday Splendor—Hobbs Thermore batting. Professionally machine-quilted by Dakota Quilt Co.

Page 90: Midnight Paths—Fabrics from Island Batiks, Star Machine Quilting thread from Coats and Fairfield Machine 60/40 Blend batting. Machine-quilted by Sandy Boobar.

Page 94: Black Tie—Fiskars rotary cutting tools and DMC quilting thread and needles.

Page 98: Prairie Garden—Gentle Flowers fabric collection by Quilt Gate for Robert Kaufman. Machine-quilted by Ginger Hayes.

Page 102: Garden Affair—Garden Affair fabric collection from Classic Cotton, Warm & Natural cotton batting from The Warm Co., Sullivan's basting spray, Dual Duty Plus all-purpose and Star Multicolored Quilting thread from Coats. Pieced with a Pfaff Creative 2140 sewing machine.

Page 106: Autumn Air—Hobbs Thermore batting. Machine-quilted by Dakota Quilt Co.

Page 110: Impulse—Impulse fabric collection from Classic Cotton, Warm & Natural cotton batting from The Warm Co. and Dual Duty Plus all-purpose and Star Multicolored Quilting thread from Coats. Machine-quilted by Tyler's Machine Quilting Service. Pieced on a Pfaff Creative 2140 sewing machine.

Page 115: Tumbling Twister—Fabrics donated by Sally's Fabrics, Mesa, Ariz. Machine-quilted by Lillian Lee.

Page 121: Rectangle Parade—Sumatra fabric collection from Blank Textiles, A Touch of Cashmere batting from the Heritage Collection by Mountain Mist and Star Machine Quilting thread from Coats. Machine-quilted by Lorraine Sweet.

Page 125: Ladies of the Lake—Fabrics from Timeless Treasures, Star Machine Quilting thread from Coats and Fairfield Machine 60/40 Blend batting. Machine-quilted by Sandy Boobar.

Page 139: Star to Star—Mirage fabric collection from Timeless Treasures, Star Machine Quilting thread from Coats and Fairfield Machine 60/40 Blend batting. Machine-quilted by Sandy Boobar.

Page 144: Stars Above—Chelsea Lane fabric collection from P&B Textiles and Hobbs Thermore batting. Machine-quilted by Dakota Quilt Co.

Page 159: X Marks the Spot—Rhapsody fabric collection from Quilting Treasures by Cranston Printworks, Cotton Blossom by Mountain Mist and Star Machine Quilting thread from Coats. Machine-quilted by Dianne Hodgkins.